HAUNTED
TELFORD

HAUNTED TELFORD

Philip Solomon

This book is dedicated to my lovely grandchildren, Liam and Elise, and with special thanks to my wife, Kath, for all her help with the production of this book

First published 2011

The History Press
The Mill, Brimscombe Port
Stroud, Gloucestershire, GL5 2QG
www.thehistorypress.co.uk

British Library Cataloguing in Publication Data.
A catalogue record for this book is available from the British Library.

ISBN 978 0 7524 5766 6
Typesetting and origination by The History Press
Printed in Great Britain

Manufacturing managed by Jellyfish Print Solutions Ltd

Contents

Do your eyes lie?

St Catherine's Church, Eyton.

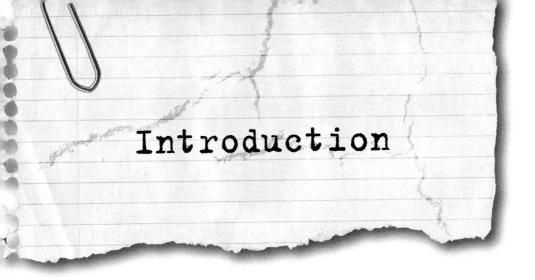

Introduction

AS in all books of this nature, perhaps the first thing to tell you about would be me. Although I was brought up in the Black Country, some of my family roots, especially on my mother's side, lie in Shropshire and Telford or Old Salop as my family preferred to call it. I suppose I am unusual in the fact that I am a psychic medium who was born to that way of life; my development as an investigator of the paranormal with the inquisitive mind I have had all my life was probably a natural progression.

I am the author of fifteen books, and have written hundreds of features over the years on all areas of the paranormal and psychic world in various newspapers and magazines and so on. For many years, I was a feature writer for *Psychic News* and at present have feature columns in *Psychic World*, *Staffordshire Advertiser*, *West Midlands Advertiser*, *Haunted* magazine and the UK's largest circulated evening newspaper, *The Wolverhampton Express & Star*. I regularly give demonstrations of clairvoyance in theatres and other venues throughout the world and often work for the UK's leading ghost hunting organisations as a specialist medium. I have been on many radio and television programmes over the years, particularly in this country and America, and also have my own radio programme on Wolverhampton City Radio.

In this book, I shall make every effort to inform you of ghost stories that have been experienced and exchanged throughout the area of Telford; a place that is considered both a modern and a new town. However, the towns, villages and land in that area are part of ancient England, its heritage and, as I hope will be proved in this book, part of its haunted history too. In this guidebook of the ghosts of Telford, all the people I have interviewed or received information from seem to be quite sure in their conviction that their stories are true and that their house, the building they speak of, or a place they have visited, is most definitely haunted. I have to say I believe these people and the ones selected for publication, in my opinion, are the truth – although of course there will always be sceptics who say such things and such experiences do not occur.

Dip into this book and you will see my reports and views of the places emerging from the stories in old and modern Telford. I would put forward the belief that it would be rather unlikely for such a large area not to have innumerable ghosts, spooks and experiences, as my understanding would suggest that every area of the UK and its cities, towns and villages, large and small, have their fair collection of spooks, spectres and other paranormal happenings – far too many to be discounted.

All things considered, it is always important to look for the normal explanation before claiming something to be paranormal, and in many of the stories in this book have done just that, giving a balanced view of what is normal and what is paranormal. One point I would like to make is that I am sure people and their opinions of the paranormal have changed greatly over the last twenty years. A lot of research suggests that many do believe in ghosts, today, or are of the opinion that there is more to life than meets the eye, and are not as embarrassed to state their opinion as they perhaps were in the past, when people tended to ridicule such beliefs.

Many programmes are now regularly broadcast about ghost hunting and, in recent years, series such as *Most Haunted* have encourged a desire in the general public to know more about ghosts and particularly to visit historic sites they are said to haunt. Many ghost books have now been written featuring just about every area of the UK and further afield; this book fits into that category as closely as possible linking right into Telford, its people, places and ghostly experiences.

The author demonstrating mediumship.

The author broadcasting his radio show.

I would always stress to not be unduly scared by the stories within or by the places it may stimulate you to want to visit. In my experience as a professional Spiritualist medium and investigator of the paranormal, I have never personally found a situation where anyone has actually been physically hurt by a ghost. However, it would be appropriate to give a little warning that you could indeed find yourself chilled as you walk the streets of new Telford and the older places where shades of yesterday are seen, heard or sensed. A medium would describe the recipient of these experiences as clairvoyant, clairaudient or clairsentient.

Those among you who have been lucky or unlucky enough to witness a paranormal experience must remember that most ghosts are just a projection of past events, and thus do not pose a tangible threat to onlookers. I often put the question to an audience of whether they have ever seen a ghost and the general response is about 20 per cent. However, when I explain that some ghosts are so lifelike that you cannot tell them from real people and then ask the question again having pointed this out to them, most people readily accept the possibility that they may have and the percentage rises incredibly much higher.

I have been truly taken aback by all the reports I have received from the people of Telford their ghost stories and experiences, whether by letter, email or by phoning into the radio programmes I have been a guest on, including Wolverhampton City Radio, BBC Radio WM and BBC Radio Shropshire. I must also give special thanks to the *Wolverhampton Express & Star* newspaper, *Shropshire Star, Shropshire Journal* and radio presenters,Keith Middleton and Danny Kelly, as they all helped greatly in enabling me to find many of the stories that are included in this book.

Telford is an eerie environment, especially at night in some of its older towns and villages, so if you are a person of a somewhat nervous disposition, you may be well advised to conduct your ghost hunts, or make your visit to some of the places mentioned in this book, during the hours of daylight. I have certainly found Telford to be one of the most haunted places I have researched in my long career. Thank you for buying this book; perhaps you will take up the challenge of investigating and judging for yourself just how haunted you consider Telford to be. Certainly, within the pages and chapters of this book you will read of ghosts a-plenty. I wish you well and hope you enjoy it. Now it is up to you to be open-minded, take pleasure from the book and make up your own mind about these stories. May all your experiences be hauntingly good ones!

Philip Solomon, 2011

1

A Brief History of Haunted Telford

TELFORD is a large new town situated in the borough of Telford and Wrekin, and is part of the ceremonial county of Shropshire, England. Telford is by far the largest town in Shropshire and continues to be one of the fastest expanding towns in the whole of the United Kingdom.

Much of modern Telford was built in the 1960s and '70s as a new town. It had originally been industrial and, previously to that, ancient agricultural land, which also included the merger of smaller places including Dawley, Oakengates, Madeley and Wellington. A large new shopping centre with an extensive shopping mall was built for the new town. The construction of the M54 motorway in 1983 linked Telford with the wider West Midlands conurbation. Telford also now includes the beautiful Ironbridge Gorge, which is a UNESCO world heritage site. The town quite rightly claims itself as

Overview of Telford Town. (Courtesy of Richard Foxcroft)

the birthplace of the industrial revolution, relevant to its proximity to Coalbrookdale and other places in the Ironbridge Gorge area, which were important to the industrial revolution and were mostly constructed on the site of the old Shropshire coalfield. The beautiful River Severn flows along its southern most boundaries.

Early settlement in the area is believed to have been on land coming up from the Weald Moors, which lay north of the town centre, towards which the famous Roman Watling Street was built. In the tenth century, extensive farmlands were relevant to three large estates, those of Lilleshall, Wrockwardine and Wellington. From the thirteenth century, much development happened in Wellington and Madeley, and Wenlock Priory founded a new town together with six monastic houses. Founded in the eleventh and twelfth centuries, they were probably very relevant to the area's economic growth and eventually acquired almost half the area, profiting greatly from coal and ironstone mining on their massive estates.

In more modern history, the new town itself was first designated thus in 1963 on 16 January as Dawley New Town, covering over 9,000 acres and including Dawley, Oakengates, Wellington, Wenlock and Shifnal rural districts. Many new homes were built for people on the Sutton Hill housing estate. A large number of new residents arrived from the West Midlands conurbations, including Birmingham, Dudley, Walsall and Wolverhampton. The commercial centre of the town is aptly named Telford Town Centre and is the home to the administration Headquarters of Telford & Wrekin Council. The extensive shopping centre and accompanying park includes the Telford Plaza, The Windsor Life Building, The Forge Retail Park and a large cinema. Telford also houses one of the Midlands' ice-skating rinks, located near to the Telford International Centre which holds conferences, concerts and many other major events. The town itself is named after Thomas Telford, the famous civil engineer, and features numerous references to this great man. Telford has many fantastic attractions to visit and, in my view, has a multitude of haunted buildings, locations and ghost stories too that have been, and continue to be, part of Telford's ancient and modern history.

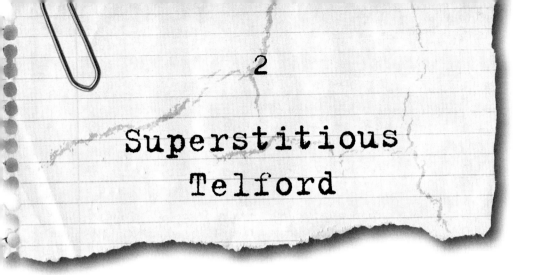

2
Superstitious Telford

Telford, like many haunted towns, plays host to a number of ancient superstitions related to ghosts and hauntings – many of which are still believed by some today. A swarm of bees around a farm or house of any family was considered an omen of impending death. A single bee entering a house was considered to be a sign that someone who lived there was about to leave this world.

It was considered extremely unfortunate to be the first person to be buried in any churchyard, as old legends suggested that such a poor individual would be making acquaintance with the Devil. Considering so many churchyards in Telford were blessed and consecrated between 1830 and 1850, one can imagine that it must have been difficult to persuade any relatives of the deceased to allow their loved ones to be the first person buried in one of them.

The older people of the area believed that the spirit of the last individual buried in a churchyard would have to remain until another burial took place before they could make their way to the other side satisfactorily.

The presence of a raven was considered particularly bad, signifying that death was about to happen; magpies in various numbers were also considered a sign of evil or bad luck.

If a bride, or in particular the bridegroom, dropped the ring as he was about to place it upon her finger, many believed that very soon a widow she would be.

Old Salopians advised strongly against naming a child after someone who had recently passed away, considering this both inappropriate and fearing that an early demise might be forthcoming for the child too.

Tolling bells were used to drive away evil spirits but if they rang unusually loudly, then a death in the vicinity was on the cards.

Shropshire and Telford people believed that a clock stopping at the moment of a person's death could mean one of two things; that the spirit had left the body of the individual or, perhaps less fortunate, that a haunting may be expected to start up very shortly.

It was considered a bad omen to stand at the bottom of someone's deathbed because the departing spirit would find it difficult to pass to the spirit world. I have to say, this is one I cannot accept.

As soon as someone passed away, all doors and windows were to be opened immediately so that the spirit could fly through the door or window and on to the higher life. However, if a wasp, bee or worse, a bird, were to fly in, then a haunting or ghostly experiences may have been about to start.

A deceased person's body must be carried feet first out of their home. Failure to follow this procedure it was believed would allegedly result in that person returning to haunt family, friends or the building itself.

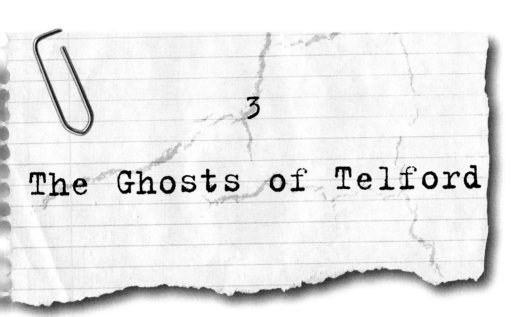

The Ghosts of Telford

I will start this chapter by telling you about a time when a Telford spectre was seen. Neither ghost nor spirit, it was instead the projection of someone who is still living.

One of the most fascinating cases I have ever investigated and written about in one of my books about ghosts, occurred in the Telford area some years ago, and was seen and reported by the most responsible of witnesses, including a senior policeman and even village dignitaries, as well as ordinary, everyday people. A lady was seen to float down the village High Street at a certain time, apparently several inches off the floor. If this was not eerie enough, she then stopped and disappeared before their very eyes.

You may say there are a million such ghost stories that have been written about in the ancient annals of Britain's history, but this one in particular had a different angle. It is suggested that this was the vision of an older lady who was actually still living in a very nice care home close to Madeley, but was her when she was much younger. It

seems that, whilst dreaming, she imagined herself walking this particular route and in some way this was projected in a physical context that could be viewed by others. I think it is particularly fascinating that it was a projection of the lady in her younger years, and I have always believed that this is an area that should be subject to far more investigation and study by parapsychologists and others.

Another example of where a spectre is neither a ghost nor spirit could be what is termed a wraith. Many years ago, especially in the Celtic countries such as Scotland and Ireland, stories were told of wraiths which were said to be the spectre or apparition of someone still alive and, if seen or viewed, would be seen as an omen that the person would shortly no longer be living in this life. Some people claim that the word wraith is an old Scottish word first mentioned in the English language in 1513, yet possibly with its roots in the ancient Norse or Viking language, where 'vordr' (their word for wraith) translates as 'warden', and was seen as a spiritual being to the Norse people.

Artist's impression of the Grey Ladies, seen throughout Telford. (Courtesy of Graham Walsh)

An artist's impression of the White Lady of Telford. (Courtesy of Graham Walsh)

Again, this was not a spirit in the context of how we would normally understand it, but the projected vision of someone still living to another person or persons, who would have this experience usually whilst in a deep sleep. In those days, people believed that this foretold the passing to the higher life of the person they had seen in their dream state. Some logic can be applied to this, for I do believe that as transference to the

Other Side draws near, the link between the physical and spiritual body weakens somewhat and their spirit may float between the two worlds.

But some reports have been made stating that even where accidental or violent death occurs, pre-warnings have been given by the appearance of wraith-like beings. This may indeed have some logic, as, in my view, the spiritual or astral body would be aware of this and be preparing for the spirit to move to the higher life. Wraiths are mentioned in several stories and books. J.R.R Tolkien in *The Lord of the Rings* novel trilogy, described wraiths as a strange form of 'undead' creatures. J.K Rowling's more recent *Harry Potter* books similarly feature wraith-like creatures that psychically draw and feed off human suffering. Some investigators of the paranormal have even suggested that a wraith is a 'shade' or ghost of an individual's emotions, and if the individual concerned dies full of anger or bad intentions, then a wraith could be a type of extreme post-death poltergeist activity, although I must say that, I do not consider this to be likely.

The Telford Puma

There are many stories of the Telford Puma of Dawley and Malinsgate, and, notably, this is one of the few cases that featured on television; but could it be that it is in fact a ghost? Surely, if it was a real non-native cat then it would have been caught

by now? Cryptozoologists do debate the possibilities that these out-of-place animals could possibly be ghosts or apparitions and that they come from other dimensions and can appear and vanish just as quickly into thin air.

An interesting historical note that I came across that was, of all places, relevant to rural France, is that cats were linked to the ancient corn harvest. The creatures would be treated with great reverence and decorated with flowers and ribbons before eventually being sacrificed. Could there be similar things that have happened in our own Telford area, which certainly many years ago was very agricultural? And could the so-called Telford Puma really be a ghost?

A Telford police report stated that on 24 November, 2006, at 3.15 a.m., an officer had seen the cat near the White Horse public house in Finger Road, Dawley. The officer described seeing an enormous black cat crossing the road and disappearing into grounds at the rear of the public house. The animal was described as being of a huge size with a long tail. Other patrols were called to the area but nothing was found to prove the sighting. By now this was the third reported incident describing a large, cat-like creature in 2006. Two Telford park rangers had also reported witnessing the presence of a large black cat very close to the town park.

PC Simmons of Telford Police, stated that sightings are rare and appear to come in clutches, giving the impression that large black cats or pumas are roaming in large numbers amongst us. Officers at the Malinsgate police station were advised to be careful when patrolling the area and many websites dedicated to such things suggest that you should be careful if you see such a creature and that, although these animals will generally avoid contact with humans and run away, you should not approach one; be calm and back away, but never run.

But the question has to be asked: if they do exist, why have they not been caught? I don't think that such excellent reports of the sightings of these animals can be rejected, but if they fall into the category of what cryptozoologists describe as possibly being from another world, or ghost-like, then in simple terms they never will be caught, will they?

The Missing Telford Girl

Yasmin Khan telephoned me regarding a story she was told by a taxi driver friend from Telford, who swears his experience was true but preferred not to name the place. However, this being such an amazing story from the Telford area, I felt that it was one ghost story that just had to be included.

One night in December 2009, during a very heavy downpour of rain, the taxi driver picked up a young girl to take her home. He guessed she was about fifteen or sixteen years of age and was wearing a mini-skirt and no coat. The girl lived at the top of the hill and it was not possible to drive up to the door of the house, so the driver, feeling sorry for her, loaned her his jacket.

A couple of days later he went back to the house to collect his coat and a man in his late sixties came to the door. The driver explained why he was there and the man disappeared into the house for a few moments and then returned to show him a picture of a blue-eyed, blonde-haired girl of about fifteen or sixteen years of age and asked if that was the girl he had seen, to which the taxi driver replied it was.

The man, who said he was the girl's father, told him she had died fourteen years before in a car crash, but that the driver's coat would most likely be in the wardrobe in the bedroom that used to belong to her, as this sort of incident had often happened since her death, and things like sweet wrappers and the like had also been found on her bed when no one had been in the room.

The man took the driver upstairs and, sure enough, hanging up in the wardrobe was his jacket. He told him, 'Make no mistake, my friend, this sort of thing happens time after time, but I am sorry for the inconvenience it has caused you and the many others it has happened to as well. But I'm at a loss as to know what to do about it!'

Priorslee Hall

Robert Jenkins contacted me about his experience whilst working at Priorslee Hall as a member of the caretaking staff for the University of Wolverhampton. This is his story ...

It would be impossible now to picture how Priorslee Hall and its environs must have looked in the centuries before the new town of Telford was conceived. Built in the early eighteenth century on an apparently virgin site, it was a family home for only a few decades before becoming the head office of the Lilleshall Mining Company, and the residence of a succession of managing directors.

With the nationalisation of the coal industry came the decline of the company's fortunes and, in about 1970, the old hall and its grounds were turned over to the Telford Development Corporation. The Corporation had no use for the gardens and cleared them in order to erect a large complex of interlinked temporary wooden (demountable) buildings. Only the stable block beside the north face of the hall survived – after modification for alternative

Priorslee Hall and caretaker's bungalow,
Telford. (Courtesy of Bob Jenkins)

Priorslee Hall and stable block, Telford. (Courtesy of Bob Jenkins)

19

use. Construction of the new town then began in earnest. To the east, the nearby Castle Farm vanished beneath an artificial lake, whilst the Old Shifnal Road was cut asunder by the Ricoh factory and the Castle Farm interchange. To the south, was constructed the M54 and, on its far side, Stafford Park industrial estate. To the north, the building of acres of new housing took place. Only in the west; were a few original buildings allowed to remain unscathed, but the old industrial and agricultural landscape was altered almost beyond recognition.

It wasn't until 1994 that I first set foot in Priorslee Hall. By then, its function had changed again and it had been taken over and refurbished by the University of Wolverhampton as the centre piece of a new campus. A host of modern teaching buildings and accommodation blocks had been constructed in the surrounding grounds and as the temporary demountable buildings had long exceeded their anticipated lifespan, they continued to serve as classrooms and offices without causing any apparent haemorrhaging of the campus maintenance budget. As a member of the caretaking staff, I worked a rotating shift pattern consisting of morning, afternoon and nightshifts in that order.

My responsibilities were manifold and varied. I covered the entire campus and opened buildings at the start of the working day or, alternatively, secured them as they were vacated by staff, and I often worked alone. Some of my colleagues disliked working alone in Priorslee Hall or in the adjacent stable block and demountables, especially when it was dark. Personally, I was lucky and had no qualms about doing so. I'd grown up in rural England, where 'dark' meant 'pitch black'. My family had also worked for the gentry and so I wasn't totally unfamiliar with stately homes and their labyrinth cellars or strange nooks. Moreover, I'd just completed a career in the Royal Military Police and knew well that life held many more tangible terrors than the supernatural. I enjoyed working on the campus as Priorslee Hall was a source of fascination for me and I found it a warm, friendly old building.

So far as I know, it held only one mystery; a tunnel discovered in the cellars when the house was renovated in 1930. A book detailing the history of the Lilleshall Mining Company relates that the tunnel led east for only a few dozen yards before the roof was found to be in a state of collapse. It was suggested that it had some relationship with Tong Priory, a few miles away, but there was no elaboration. Most stately homes are built on the site of earlier dwellings, but that does not seem to have been the case at Priorslee. However, secret passages are often associated with the religious strife and persecution of the Elizabethan era and earlier, which might indicate that the tunnel was older than the hall and the remnant of some previous building. At the far end of the kitchen, an open doorway on the right led into a short corridor that dog-legged to the left. At the end of that was a door leading into a long corridor that ran the length of the building between the stairwells, and looked out upon a grassed quadrangle that possessed half a dozen mature fruit trees. It was in this corridor that I was to witness two unexplainable events which occurred years apart and in different forms.

My training as a military investigator taught me that a fact is something ascertained by one or more of the five senses, sight, sound, smell, touch and taste. The things I witnessed were not the manifestations of poor mental or physical health, or external influences. On both occasions, I was alone, but untroubled, in the quiet and empty building when my senses were at their most receptive. I know what I heard and saw, and my inability to link those events to a rational explanation has irritated me ever since.

Having finished my task, I was walking up the long corridor to leave the building via the kitchen exit. At the end of the corridor in front of me was a door to the stairwell and, immediately to the left of that, the door into the short hallway leading to the kitchen. There was no one on campus except for myself, my mate, and the site superintendent, who lived with his family in a bungalow behind the stables, and their home had been in darkness when I had passed it earlier.

As I approached the end of the corridor, I clearly heard someone ascending the stairs behind the door ahead. The steps were unhurried and assuming that it was my friend up to his tricks again, I paused to listen as the door at the top of the stairs was casually opened and closed. If the wooden doors and stairs hadn't been so prone to creaking and squeaking, I would have attempted to steal up on him stealthily and spring my own surprise, but that was impossible, so I set out to spoil his fun as quickly as possible by exposing him.

I rapidly passed through the door and up the stairs. Through the door at the top of the stairs was a corridor that ran to the far end of the building, with empty rooms to the left and right of it. I half expected to see my friend in the corridor, but having made my own noise climbing the stairs it was quite possible that he had been able to dart into one of the empty rooms without me hearing his movements. I thus bellowed out my intention of catching him and proceeded along the corridor, checking the rooms as I went. I had been trained to be alert and thorough in such matters and I missed nothing, but by the time I reached the other end of the corridor, I still hadn't found him and the door into the stairwell was locked. The lock was stiff and how he had managed to evade me without my noticing him was astonishing.

I admitted defeat and called him on the radio that I carried, asking him where he was. He replied that he was in Reception. That was located in the centre of the campus, nowhere close to SJ block, so I called him a liar and repeated my question, but when he replied that time, I suddenly realised that I could hear a transistor radio playing in the background. We had one in Reception that we listened to at night. Sensing something was amiss, he asked me if I was alright. I was, but I replied truthfully that I'd heard somebody moving around in SJ block. He asked me if I wanted him to phone the police, but I replied that I didn't, because I'd checked the building and hadn't found anything suspicious.

When I returned to Reception a few minutes later, my mate's initial curiosity turned to mirth as he teased me for imagining things and I didn't think about it much thereafter, although when the story was passed on to the cleaning ladies – at my expense – a couple of them were less dismissive than others and stated that they'd never really liked working in SJ when it was used formerly as offices, because it had made them feel strangely uncomfortable. One said that she always felt as though someone was watching her.

Advancing four years and I was still in the same role, but much more knowledgeable about it. One March evening, after the demountables complex had been vacated by staff and students, I checked and secured it. It was still early evening, about 7 p.m.,

but it was dark and I completed my check of the buildings by walking around the outside, looking for any open windows or lights still left on. I found that all was well, except that the external security lights on SJ block hadn't come on. They were activated by a timer that was meant to switch them on and off automatically, but when that failed it necessitated someone having to enter the building via the maintenance kitchen, silence the alarm and then go to a cupboard under the stairs by the caretaker's storeroom in order to press a button that would override the timer. I did that, switching the ceiling lights on as I went rather than walking through the place in darkness.

As I retraced my steps via the long corridor, at a point almost exactly where I had been when I had heard footsteps previously, I saw a football-sized sphere of grey vapour enter the corridor at head height through the door that led from the maintenance department on my left. It then passed immediately through the door at the end of the corridor in front of me. The expression, 'I couldn't believe my eyes!' means just that. My brain was greatly confused. I was only three or four yards from the object and the lighting was good. The data had been gathered, but it made no sense; none at all. I didn't feel any different; I was a bit startled, but not frightened and rather keen to follow up what I'd seen, so I immediately opened the door in front of me, but all I found was the darkened and quiet stairwell.

I know hearing footsteps is supposed to be quite common, but I was surprised to discover that the phenomenon of vaporous spheres is also quite common and has been filmed. Most of these are red spheres however, which are thought to represent anger. The one I saw was simply opaque and caused me no alarm. My instinct was to believe that the things I witnessed were echoes of some event which had involved a great emotional energy. I feel strongly that the sort of event behind my experiences could have been someone going to an office up the stairs whilst feeling increasingly unwell, and being aware that death was imminent.

Blists Hill Museum

Mr and Mrs McCarthy had a most unusual ghostly experience while visiting the Blists Hill Museum for a special evening around the time of Halloween one year. The event had been designed to set up illusions of such spooky things. Perhaps primed by the name of the event, Blists Hill Ghostly Gaslight, the couple were expecting to see unusual things that evening, but certainly not to meet a real ghost, which they feel quite sure they did.

Walking past the chemist's shop in the High Street, they saw a gentleman of about fifty-five dressed in an old-fashioned frock coat that farmers used to wear in the Telford and Shropshire areas. In his mouth, he had a very long, white clay pipe and carried an exceptionally long stick or stave. 'You would have taken him for a real person', said Mary, 'Except that looking down at the ground he had no feet or ankles, and, more incredibly than that,' remarked Michael, 'he walked through a nearby wall.'

The couple, in their words, were 'gob smacked'. It was the most incredible special effect you could imagine, and moving a little further down the street they asked a staff member how such a thing was possible. The member of staff looked them straight in the eye and said they had no idea what they were talking about or what had happened, and that no one was in such a costume on duty that evening; in fact, it would not fit in with the historical setting of the museum at all. The couple were sensible, honest people in my view, and I think the only conclusion that can be drawn is that they had indeed seen a ghost or spirit that evening. Perhaps the Blists Hill Museum has been created on a higher level than farmland, perhaps it has been built on from another time. This would certainly explain the spectre having no feet; he was basically walking on a lower level.

There was also an unusual ghost story that happened one Bonfire Night. Many people attend a communal bonfire at the museum and, on one occasion, according to Mr Gripton who was visiting with his family, an old-fashioned fairground was set up. Mr Gripton found himself separated from his family and became engaged in conversation with a very interesting man who introduced himself as Joe. In his own words, Mr Gripton was fascinated by the stories Joe told him about the fairgrounds of yesteryear, and particularly about how some of the items had been restored.

Rejoining his family, he told them of the conversation he had had with Joe and decided he would go back to the fairground area to ask about the possibility of writing to the gentleman in question with regard to him sending his information on to one of the local newspapers. When he made enquiries about Joe to the staff manning the fair, no one knew who he was talking about or describing. Did Mr Gripton have a conversation with a ghost that evening? He is quite sure he did, and from how he described his experience to me I have to say I believe him.

Telford Shopping Centre

Karen Westwood told me a very interesting story about the Telford Shopping Centre that had been related to her by her friend who still works there. At one time, while studying at university, he had obtained a part-time job in the centre itself. He told her many people used to report the very strange experience of seeing people dressed in clothing of the Norman period of occupation, both in the centre and the town park. Fascinated by the continual reports, a little research suggested that at one time the shopping centre had actually been built on the remains of an ancient Norman building which had eventually been moved to the town park.

Could these ancient people still be walking around? We know that energies from other times can be drawn into the fabric of buildings and cause a haunting-type experience, similar to what Karen's friend described. A little further investigation by me also suggests that others have seen people of yesteryear including people from the Saxon times. Is the centre built on a portal that creates this type of experience, time-slip, ghosts, and so on? It certainly is a possibility, is it not?

The Princess Royal Hospital

The Princess Royal Hospital, Telford, is a modern and well-appointed hospital that serves the people well, with 330 beds, surgical operations and an excellent maternity unit all available. There will certainly be stories of ghosts in all hospitals, old and new, but the story told to me by Andy and Liz concerns the front of the building, and has nothing to do with the inside at all. The couple had been travelling in the vicinity and saw what they thought had been a road accident. Although no people were to be seen

physically, it looked to be an old-fashioned motorcycle with a combination side-car on the side that had run into the kerb.

Driving round the old combination vehicle and into the car park, they went into the reception area and reported what they had seen, but were told by the staff that they knew nothing of such an incident. So they went back to have another look and discovered nothing at all was to be seen of their former vision. Andy, who is a more modern biker, was adamant that even in the fleeting view of the old bike, it couldn't have been ridden away. Did they see a replay of an incident from years before? It is certainly a possibility.

Princess Royal Hospital Entrance.

Telford Churchyards

Many churchyards have reports of animal ghosts such as dogs and cats, but a most unique report in Telford is that of pigs and sheep. Many people have reported seeing such creatures that vanish before their eyes or have been seen in their peripheral vision. But this is not that surprising, for most of the churchyards in the Telford area during Victorian times, and prior to that, were surrounded by fields and farm buildings, and research suggests that pigs and sheep were allowed to graze or eat the brush and grass around the graves and church, and did a very good job keeping the graveyards from becoming overgrown. The 1895 Church Warden's Guide clearly states that there should be no objection of sheep grazing in the churchyards or burial grounds generally.

Many churchyards are built on the site of pagan pre-Christian sites. Dawley's Holy Trinity Church and Wellington's All Saint's Parish Church are said to stand on earlier sites of pagan activity, so the story told to me by two middle-aged ladies, Christine and Sheila, is not surprising. When they were teenagers, the pair saw three men that looked like Vikings near the Dawley church, giving extremely accurate descriptions, but being very surprised that they didn't have the horns on their helmets that one would expect. Of course, we now know today that these Norse visitors never did have horns on their helmets; this detail is something that had possibly been described by monks or other leaders of the native Britons to suggest that the Vikings were more devilish than they really were, so that the Saxons would fight even more bitterly.

Albrighton Railway Station

Members of the Lycett family, long-time residents of Telford, told me the story of

Railway bridge, Albrighton.

David Austen Roses, Albrighton.

the haunting of Albrighton railway station, where many members of their family used to get off the train before making their way to places such as Shifnal, Madeley, and so on. Their story happened during the Second World War, when a young man who had been serving with the Air Force arrived late at the station on the very last train. He was surprised to see a lady dressed in fine garments walking up and down the platform, distraught and obviously upset. 'Are you alright?' he asked. 'Of course I am!' she snapped back, 'I'm waiting for my husband.' She then stuck her nose in the air and walked away. This is where things got really spooky, for, in the young man's words, she simply vanished into thin air. This man was not the first or last to tell of this occurence, but he was the only person she was supposed to have ever actually spoken to, this posh lady who, unfortunately it seems, waits for a train and husband that never arrive.

As an addition to this story, a member of my own family, while serving in the Air Force regiment, also saw the lady although she did not speak to him. As someone who is fascinated by this subject, I can only say how unlucky he was. But he probably wouldn't agree with this, it must be said!

Cosford Airfield

Christine, who used to live in Birkenhead, told me an intriguing story about when she moved to the area in the early 1960s. She was about eighteen or nineteen at the time and lived with her boyfriend and two small children in a two-berth caravan, close to the David Austin Roses Nursery (now called Boningale Nurseries), in a little lane off the Old Worcester Road, that ran along the edge of the Cosford Airfield. Opposite the field where the caravan was sited, there was a row of cottages where one couple she remembers, who were called Mr and Mrs Lamb, lived, and also some allotments, and so on.

Christine says there used to be what was called a thrift shop on the land belonging to Cosford Airfield, close to the married quarters where she often went to buy clothes for her family. One evening, as it was dropping dusk, she was on her way back from the shop, when, heading straight towards her, was an old-style stagecoach with no driver. She had to move out of the way very quickly as it rumbled past, but as she turned round to get a better look, it disappeared completely. When she told a friend about it later, they said it was common knowledge that a highwayman had cut the throat of a stagecoach driver many years before and that other people had also seen this stagecoach go by.

Christine also said there was a firegrate with a small wood/coal burner in the caravan, with a door at the front that opened to put the wood, and so on in. It was quite tricky to open and you needed to use both hands to do so, but it inexplicably often used to just swing open on its own and then slam shut again, which she found very unnerving. She said that nothing seemed to go right while they lived there and she felt as though they were being driven away.

Christine and her partner eventually split up and lost contact with each other, but she believes he may have moved back to his native Scotland. As the children got older, they wanted to know more about their father and wished to find him if possible. Christine tried to find out more by contacting the former owners of the land and site where they had lived in the caravan. But, try as she might, no one seemed to remember the field with the caravan or the cottages and allotments that were opposite, which had all disappeared. On top of that there seemed to be no records kept of these places either and she was told, 'There has never been buildings, houses or anything else on this land.' Christine says she is absolutely mystified as to how no one can recall anything about the area or the records that must have made and kept at the time.

Allscott

I came across a very interesting story of a Telford lorry driver, Garry from Trench, a man who had regularly gone rambling through the country areas of Allscott for many years. His experience was of seeing an old man dressed in an old Salopian milking gown, who then proceeded to dissolve into thin air before his very eyes. Garry had this experience close by the former sugar beet factory and had walked the area many times as a boy in the company of his uncle, doing quite a bit of rabbiting in the area. He still takes his dogs there for walks today and this is where he had his more modern-day vision. It had been on a Sunday at around 5.30 p.m. as they walked close to the factory. One of his dogs began barking and he looked up to see what had caught its attention. There was an elderly man dressed in a long, brown-coloured gown, the sort of thing that would have been used by cow keepers and farmers for milking cows in years gone by. He was also wearing the traditional flat cap. Garry spoke to him and said, 'Alright?' But the man just looked back without replying. Walking on a short distance, Garry picked up the dog and looked back, but nowhere was anyone at all to be seen.

Apley Wood & Wappenshall Hamlet

Philip Childs phoned with a story his grandfather had told him some years ago when he was a child. Philip's grandparents at one time lived at the Apley cottages in Apley Wood by the main road, which at one time used to be no more than a country lane. Philip's grandfather and uncle worked on a nearby farm and had been told that in the Wappenshall Hamlet, a baby had been murdered many years before and appears every year on the anniversary of its murder at the T-Junction at the nearby site known as 'the stony stile'. No one, including Philip, really knows the background to this, but this is certainly the sort of situation where the victim of murder will recreate some sort of replay in the ether that those of a sensitive nature might witness.

One can only wonder if there is some special reference to 'the stony stile' site that causes this vision to occur. Could it be that this is where the murder took place? Or perhaps where those relevant to the birth of the child had met? Or maybe even the baby was buried in that vicinity somewhere. Philip couldn't give a great deal of information about this story, but I do find it a fascinating and spooky tale.

The Red Pool of Benthall Edge

Close to Benthall Edge, and not far from the power station, is the place of a most unusual pool. People have claimed that the waters have turned red in front of the eyes of those who are sensitive to such things. There is a story locally that the cause of such paranormal activity relates to when a young woman was violated and then slain by a group of workers from the nearby limestone works, who then threw her weighted and bleeding body into the depths of the water. Others have said they have repeatedly seen a young man who stands by the water's edge, wringing his hands and looking left and right, and is claimed to be the fiancé searching for his poor Mary, who unfortunately would never be found, not living at least. The young man is known to some as Poor David.

The Trapped Man of Benthall Edge

A very interesting story was told of a gentleman of the Victorian era, 'Gaffer' as they called them back then, carrying the wages to be paid to the workers at the limestone works on Benthall Edge. There are those who say he was attacked by robbers who knew the path he would walk. They tied him up, gagged him and took the cash, before chucking him down a pit, over which they then rolled a very large stone. Legend has it that his shouts for help would never have

been heard – even if he had been able to remove the gag – as the constant din from nearby industrial workings would muffle any cries for help. The poor man was eventually declared missing and a search party was organised. Tremendous efforts were made to find him, including the eventual removal of the stone, where it appears he may have broken free, but was then smashed to death when the stone had fallen deeper into the pit and down upon his body. There is not the same amount of industry now to cover the sounds of the cries for help, and many who walk in this area today report hearing someone shouting for help, which seems to reverberate along Benthall Edge and from the claimed site of the pit.

Benthall Hall

I came across a very interesting story about a lady who had been a housekeeper at the hall for many years, before being made redundant when new tenants took up residence there. It appears that over the years this lady had met many visitors and one day, while she was doing reception duty, a couple who must have been in their fifties told her of a strange experience they had just had while sitting on a bench in the gardens.

Apparently they had been spoken to by a young girl who they described as being very pretty and with a lovely smile, who had asked them if they liked her garden. They were also rather surprised and puzzled as to why she seemed to be dressed

Benthall church.

in clothes of another time. As the couple were about to enter into conversation with her, she simply dissolved away into nothing. The couple were adamant that they had never really believed in the paranormal and ghosts, and found the very idea of their existence quite humorous. They were not scared of such things at all. They also said that this was, indeed, an experience they had enjoyed very much and one they would always remember.

The housekeeper at the hall reported that there had been many others who had seen the pretty little girl in the gardens, but, rather sadly for her, she had never had the experience of viewing her. She said that she was always very comfortable, contented and happy there, but did think that you could almost feel the presence of children laughing and playing on occasions. There had certainly been many children who had resided there throughout the history of the building. One family of Benthall Hall is reported to have had twenty children, and the Maws family who had at one time resided there, also had many children, several dying at a young age, including a little girl who was laid to rest in the churchyard of the nearby beautiful Benthall church and whose grave can be found there to this day.

Could this be the charming little girl who still loves to visit the gardens at Benthall? Is this the pretty child with the delightful smile who appears to visitors to the hall? I think this is a particularly lovely story of what may be a spirit visitation rather than a ghostly haunting .

Brookside

Candice saw a most unusual object in the sky, which she described as being a strange basket shape. I take the view that unidentified flying objects (UFOs) are a different thing to ghosts altogether. In fact, I have come to the conclusion that when we consider how vast the universe is, visitors and crafts from other planets over the years is rather more likely than unlikely. Certainly Telford has had its share of such experiences and there is even the story of UFOs and aliens actually landing at Cosford some years ago. But that would really be more appropriately researched, discussed and talked about for a possible book in the future on UFOs – or close encounters of the first kind, if you like! However, some people would say that what Candice described in the sky is similar to the unusual shapes that are considered to be ghostly-type energies seen and experienced on the ground, such as misty shapes, vapours and similar spectral objects.

Broseley Church

Jenny Davis had a strange experience while visiting Broseley church. She was looking at the old gravestones against one of the walls when she suddenly felt quite dizzy and that her head was spinning. She'd had a heavy cold for over a week and felt that this must be the cause, but as she peered more closely at one of the gravestones, she saw what she thought was the face of an elderly lady. Blinking, this faded away. She turned to walk away, and going to the road area of the churchyard she saw a lady in old-fashioned clothes who looked very like the person she had seen on the gravestone.

Returning to her home in Highley, she told her mother of the experience she'd had and was told that the lady she described was very much like her great grandmother, who had indeed been buried at Broseley churchyard. The next day, both

ladies returned to the churchyard but could not find the gravestone at all. Did Jenny have a paranormal experience and see the vision of her great grandmother? I feel it is a ghostly possibility that cannot be discounted.

UFOs in Broseley

Julie had a very strange experience of seeing two boomerang-shaped lights just above her home. Were they of a paranormal nature, ghosts, shades or possibly even UFOs? I don't know whether UFOs should be listed in a ghost book, but certainly Telford over the years has been one of those hotspot places for strange visions in the sky and the like, and there are certainly people who have hypothesised the view that they could be a ghostly energy.

Broseley Wood

Edinburgh House has its fair share of spooks and things that go bump in the night. Mildred, a tiny, thin lady, middle-aged and with a very large key that swings from her waist, has been seen within various parts of the building. There have also been reports of hooded monks seen in and around the area. This is entirely possible as Edinburgh House itself is partly attached to an old chapel which had included burial grounds. Jack Linley informed me that his father told him he often saw unusual lights or the sight of strange rising gases in this area.

An unusual orb photgraph taken by the author at a
haunted site. The orb was pink rather than the usual white colour.

Many people today take photographs that show orbs or lights similar to this, but of course in Jack Linley's father's day such cameras were not available. Other people have also told me that they have seen little golden balls, strange lights and unusual mists, so this might be a good area to take a few pictures on your modern digital cameras. Older people from Broseley Wood also tell of the spirit of an old lady in the town who has spoken to people, and of a tall male that is seen holding the head of a long-haired woman, and also of a woman's screams that send shivers down the strongest of spines!

Buildwas Abbey

The abbey itself was built in 1135 and was for many years the home of Cistercian monks. Legend has it that the monks built a rude and basic crossing over the River Severn which stood for many years and served greatly the people of both sides of the river. It is little wonder then that the sounds of monks saying their prayers or chanting are often heard in the vicinity of the building and, strangely enough, even on the famed Iron Bridge of today. Residents also speak of the ghost of the Black Abbot, who is alleged to have been slain by assassins unknown, perhaps relevant to a vendetta or religious disagreement.

Buildwas Power Station

Workers have described unusual sounds of moaning and shouting in this area that appear to come from no physical source, but there are also stories of a hooded monk,

Buildwas Abbey.

known as the Black Abbot, and strangely of miners with dirty black faces. Notably. coal was transported to the building right up until 1969 from the Highley Mine. People have also spoken of the sound of galloping and whinnying horses, and the loud cracking sound of a whip, accompanied by a male voice that shouts, 'Clearway! Clearway!' A very unusual and alarming experience when it just randomly comes out of the air towards you, with nothing visual to be seen at all, quite simply an audible experience.

Cluddley

Carol Sharp told me a very unusual story about an event that happened to her and her family in Cluddley. She said that back in 1992 she and her husband and daughter moved into a cottage in Cluddley (on the Wellington side of the Wrekin). During the two weeks prior to moving in, her husband, Tony, redecorated throughout and, whilst up a ladder, felt a presence watching him –but there was absolutely no one else in the house.

That was just the start of many incidents during their six years living there. Upstairs there was a long landing that went the whole width of the house and every time their daughter walked along the landing to go from the bathroom back to her bedroom, she felt something trying to push her down the stairs (the stairs were in the middle of the landing and she felt nothing either side of the stairs at all). The dogs also used to sit on the half landing, looking up the stairs and occasionally growling as if someone was walking by. Several times

whilst alone in the house Tony could hear footsteps on the landing, but Carol never had any of these experiences felt by her daughter and husband.

However, their son, who was at college and never really lived in the house, was moving to America for six months as part of his course and had to bring all his belongings back to them to keep while he was away. The day before he left, they packed all his belongings into closed boxes and put everything into the small bedroom that he used to use when he came home. His shoes were all packed into a box with a lid; his seaman's hat (he had been in the sea scouts as a boy and had kept his hat) was on top of the box of shoes, and a teddy bear from his girlfriend was placed on top of a shelf in the corner of the room.

The morning after Jonathan left for the States, Carol woke up to find their bedroom door open, which was something that happened quite often so that didn't really bother her. But, when she went onto the landing, she noticed that the small bedroom door was also open. This was something that had never happened before,

so she went in to investigate. Carol says she was amazed to find that all of their son's shoes were now out of the box and lined up along the wall in pairs, and the lid to the box they were in was back on the box. The sea hat that was formerly on top of the box was now on the head of the teddy bear on the other side of the room. No one had been into that room since Jonathan had left and they never found an explanation for why his things had been moved around.

Carol says that she and her husband had never felt threatened in any way by a presence, and their daughter was the only one who had seemed to suffer any aggression, but they did have friends who often came over for the evening or for dinner but would never stay the night, preferring to get a taxi home and returning the following morning to collect their car.

Coalbrookdale Ironworks

Rosehill House today is part of the living museum of Ironbridge Gorge, but at one time had been the residence of Richard Ford, who was the manager of the famous Coalbrookdale Ironworks. The house itself was owned by Abraham Darby's family, who were Quakers, simple and strict in their lifestyle, but who had servants, fitting of their high-standing within the community.

No one really knows who the old lady is that sits in a rocking chair in the kitchen area, or the identity of the gentleman in top hat and silver stick who walks in and around the building and whose presence is often known by the sound of his tap, tap, tapping on the floors. Some residents say this is a sign Mr Dick is around again, so perhaps this is the gentleman in the top hat.

Some girls who visited there years ago were quite adamant that during their

The old bosses' houses at Coalbrookdale.

Ironbridge.

35

visit someone pinched their bottoms and touched their hair. Staff have also reported sensing the energy of an amorous gentleman, but by and large there seems no real harm in this particular spirit.

Coalbrookdale

Today, the old warehouse building serves as a library and office facility for the Ironbridge Gorge Museum, but legend has it that it is the site where a boy was crushed to death in an accident involving moving iron with ropes and chains. People say here is where you will find a very cold building on occasions and, in quieter moments, the terrifying sound of a lad crying out for his father or desperately shouting for help to someone or something unknown.

Mr Hallmark told me of his experience many years ago when someone used to tug at his coat, or when the building was quiet and empty, he would hear the sound of something crashing but no object was ever to be found.

It has to be said that accidents like the one mentioned above often cause ghostly replays of this nature in the ether, and this may well be the reason why people have this experience here.

Cosford

It is worth paying a visit to the Aerospace Museum at Cosford; there are aeroplanes and lots of other things of great interest to be seen there, but perhaps the most famous story is of the RAF bomber plane that comes with its own ghost known as Bill.

The plane was purchased by the museum in 1978 and, shortly after this, a visitor to the museum took a picture of the aircraft, which clearly showed an unexplained spectre sitting in the cockpit wearing clothes from the war years. Later that year, one of the staff claimed they had seen things moving in the plane, and that the lighting gear switched itself on and off, and strange noises were coming from the plane itself which were described as sounding like a crash-landing. Also, the temperature seemed to change around the area and some people have reported seeing other unexplained military-type figures which are not of modern times or, indeed, anyone who would have been authorised to be there by the museum.

In truth, no one seems to know for sure who the ghost of this aeroplane might be, and the craft itself was built too late to have seen war service, its history suggesting this Lincoln RF398 Lindholme Bomber had been manufactured in Yorkshire, probably in the late 1950s. The only records that can be found of an accident with such a plane is one that happened at Hatfield Moor.

Some people feel that there may be some relevance to this incident, as it is the only remaining plane of its kind to have survived. Could it be, because of the type of plane it is, there is an energy return and replay of that crash that draws it towards the museum?

Many paranormal organisations have had a great deal of interest in this haunted bomber and have written their own reports about it, and one fact that can be stated is that the plane itself has certainly seen some strange paranormal goings-on.

Dawley

Pauline and Debbie emailed me with a story of their experiences in a shop they haven't long moved into in High Street, Dawley, called Sheer Elegance. They have turned it into a training academy for beauty, holistic treatment and spiritual

Cosford Aerospace Museum.

awareness, and since moving in have had many experiences which they can't explain.

There is a strong energy in the building which, although not unpleasant, feels different downstairs compared to upstairs. The man who owned the shop before Pauline and Debbie took it over had a brother who used the upstairs as living quarters; it had a bedroom and a small living and kitchen area. Although a non-believer and sceptic of the paranormal, he says that he often got the impression there was a child up there, although he never saw it. He also used to hang his clothes on the door to the bedroom and very often they seemed to blow backwards and forwards as though someone had brushed past them.

He became so convinced that this was the spirit of a little girl, that he even bought a doll for her to play with!

The two ladies also felt the presence of what they thought seemed to be a little girl and they asked a medium to go to the shop to see if she could pick up what the energy was that they were experiencing. She said it was a little girl who appeared to be from the Victorian era and was wearing a white dress. She sits on the stairs but doesn't come into the downstairs rooms. Pauline and Debbie say they had noticed that there is an energy in the downstairs rooms, but about halfway up the stairs the energy changes and feels different upstairs. They say they are not unpleasant energies but they are very strong.

Debbie says that a couple of nights after the medium had been to the shop, about 3 a.m. in her own home, her young daughter – who was sleeping with her – woke up and said she had seen a little girl with black hair and a white top picking up some teddy bears that had been placed on the floor and had put them on the bed. Sure enough, when Debbie checked, the teddies were indeed on top of the bed. Her daughter wasn't afraid but was very wide awake and was able to describe the little girl in detail, finishing with, 'But I couldn't see her trousers, Mummy!'

Other strange happenings at the shop include the room they call the 'spiritual room', where they keep a crystal ball on a shelf. Time and again when they go into the room, they find the ball has been placed under a particular chair. Neither they, nor the staff, put it there and it is impossible for it to roll off the shelf onto the floor. So one can only assume it must be ghostly hands that place it under the seat! They also experience the lights being switched on and off every day between about 9.30 and 10 a.m. and again at around 11 a.m. One day when the light went out and didn't come back on, they actually found the wall switch in the off position when they went to switch the light back on themselves!

Pauline says that one morning she came into the premises through a side door and went into one of the rooms. She heard someone come in through the same entrance not long after, who she presumed to be another member of staff, but when she

Sheer Elegance, Dawley.

went to see who it was, there was no one in the building.

In one of the rooms downstairs they often see shadows of what look like people very fleetingly, and, when they took some photographs in one of the upstairs rooms after refurbishing it, they found lots of unexplained orbs on the pictures.

The Swan Hotel, Dawley

David Jones told me of the family story he had heard concerning the Swan Hotel. Apparently, at one time the building had served as a stagecoaching inn, and this would probably explain why one of his uncles had seen a very tall man, wearing a leather apron and carrying keys.

Another ghost that is said to make his presence felt at the Swan is a gentleman spectre, who is reportedly claimed to replace objects that have been knocked over, straightens picture frames, locks and unlocks doors and is described by some as the butler, although there is no particular reason for this, and by others as Mr Humphrey.

It is also claimed that dogs do not sit comfortably with the spirits of the Swan Hotel, and it is not unusual for them to growl or for their hair to stand on end as they fix their eyes on something generally unseen by humans.

Peggy, the cook, told an interesting story. At one time, when she had been walking on one of the landings at the Swan, she saw a man in a very long, dark coat and wearing

Swan Hotel, Dawley.

trousers that looked like rough leather. Some people believe this figure may be of a traveller or a wealthy Romany who was slain and had all his money and possessions stolen in one of the bedrooms in the building about 150 years ago.

To this day there are those who say slow, heavy footsteps are heard that move in the direction of the door of one particular bedroom, and then stop just as quickly when reaching their destination. The Swan Hotel, for sure, is reported as being a very haunted old building.

The Queen's Head, Dawley

The Queen's Head in King Street is a nice little pub that has always been popular with the locals and has a reputation for being friendly, but, unfortunately, this was not the case for a group of young lads a few years ago.

Admittedly, in their own words, they'd had a few drinks in a few other pubs that night. Making their way to the Queen's Head around 10 p.m. and having a round of drinks, they were warned by the barman that he would be closing the doors at 10.30 p.m. and true to his word, at 10.25 p.m., he asked them sharply to, 'Drink up and leave the premises!'

As they made their way out of the pub, they were passed by a man in unusual leather clothes making his way inside. They paused for a second and then decided that if someone else was going to be served then they would too and banged on the door to be let in, only to be told to go away and that no one at all had entered. One of the lads, coming to his senses, pointed out to the others, 'You know what, fellas, I think we've just seen a ghost!'

Queen's Head, Dawley.

The Ghostly Miners of Dawley

The ghosts of three young miners are regularly seen walking in and around the area, singing and supporting the lad in the middle, an unusual ghostly sighting. So real a vision has appeared that some people have thought it was actors or three young men dressed up in fancy dress, but this opinion has gone out of the window once they have dissolved and disappeared in front of witnesses. Some people believe they are the ghosts of three young men who died at the Ketley coal pit around 1850, and their deaths may have been less than accidental in some way.

The Haunted Memorial, Dawley

In the High Street stands a memorial to Captain Webb, the first person to swim the English Channel and who eventually lost his life in a failed attempt to swim across Niagara Falls. The brave captain lies buried in the nearby Oakwood cemetery. A most unusual ghost story links to this memorial; a young man in an officer's uniform relevant to the First World War, who walks up towards the memorial, stops a few feet short and salutes before simply fading away. Could it be a relative of the great swimmer? Or perhaps a young man who saw Webb as a hero and continues to pay the same respect to him as he did in the living years, with a manly and respectful salute?

Captain Webb's statue, Dawley.

The Slaughter Pit of Donnington Wood

A group of men and a horse from another time have been seen running through the area of Donnington Wood and may be relevant to an accident known locally as the slaughter pit. A dozen miners and a horse had all plunged to their death whilst being lowered into the pit early one morning and this is just the sort of occurrence that would cause a haunting to happen over and over again. But why they are collectively running is hard to understand, unless their thoughts were of escaping in some way at the final moment of their death.

The Old Man of Donnington Wood

Several people have reported the sight of an old man, who walks past them and brings a cold energy and sense of something being wrong. When people turn round the old gent appears to do so too, but alarmingly with a severed or cut throat. No one knows the reason behind this frightening vision and most people don't hang around to ask, although some give the nickname of Bloody John or Isaiah to this particular grisly ghost or spirit.

Doseley, Home to the Heaviest Man in Shropshire

The churchyard in Doseley was where one of Shropshire's heaviest men was finally laid to rest. William Ball, although only around 5ft 8in was alleged to have weighed over 40 stone and was well known at the Coalbrookdale Company at the Horsehay Works. He died in 1852 but many people have spoken of the huge man in top hat, bright waistcoat and stick that has appeared in and around Doseley, particularly close to the old viaduct and the churchyard itself. They call him Big Billie. But could it be the ghost of William Ball? This seems to be a likely possibility.

Eyton on the Weald Moors

A lady phoned into Radio Shropshire when I was the special guest of my good friend Keith Middleton, a man who is always very fair and open to the possibility of ghosts and the paranormal on his excellent radio shows. This lady told us a very unusual story about Eyton Hall Stables where, at one time in her younger life, she had witnessed the vision of two men in top hats who appeared from nowhere.

Doseley Viaduct, the possible location of spectral sightings of William Ball. (Courtesy of Richard Foxcroft)

The Highwayman of Hadley

Looking at old pictures, she felt they would have been footmen or coach drivers, perhaps returning on special occasions to check the horses or coaches from times long since committed to history. She didn't give the exact location and when we asked about this she said she would rather not say, but she had obviously been very alarmed by her experience.

I have a feeling that she may well have seen a vision of her own ancestors from yesteryear, and this seemed to be a reccurring theme throughout the radio interview. Many people, in Telford particularly, seem to have this ability to see and sense the other world, and I have long come to the conclusion that people from certain parts of the world and certain places do seem to have more of this ability than others.

Suzanne had a very unusual story to tell of when her family lived in the Haybridge Road area of Hadley, concerning horse-drawn carriages that sped by on occasions. Other people would speak of the sounds of horses' hooves and the sound of men calling out to others. But perhaps the most fascinating story of all was of the highwayman that others have also spoken of in the vicinity, which on one particular occasion was seen by Suzanne's father, when the ghost turned and fired his pistol at him.

One can only be grateful that ghostly bullets, or pistol shot, to be more correct, cannot harm or injure, but it is certainly one of the most incredible stories of interaction between the two worlds, perhaps the spirit of the highwayman was returning to do his

Highwayman (Courtesy of Graham Walsh.

Hadley. (Courtesy of Richard Foxcroft)

dastardly deeds, if not in the physical sense then certainly in spirit.

The Ghost Dog of Horsehay

A lady from Horsehay in Telford wrote to me about a very strange experience she and her partner had driving back home one night during the summer of 2008 after visiting their son. She says they had turned left off the Espley roundabout onto the A442 road towards Telford at about 11.40 p.m., which in places is quite narrow but at that time of night was quite deserted. The headlights were on full so they could see quite well ahead of them and also along the verges which are lined with hedges, wire and ditches in some parts along the way.

In the distance, the lady's partner noticed a car approaching and dipped his headlights. As the car drew near, a very large dog appeared from out of nowhere in front of their car. Her partner braked hard and swerved, hoping not to hit the dog or the approaching car, and they braced themselves for some sort of collision with either or both, – but it never happened because the dog and the car just vanished, apparently into thin air. She says they never came to a complete halt and were nervous to stop as they were unsure of what had just happened and, as one would imagine, they were both shaken and astounded. They asked each other what had just happened, but on reaching home, as they were both very tired and just feeling thankful that they were still in one piece, they went to bed to get some sleep.

Horsehay.

It was the next day that they really started questioning the events of the night before. They both agreed that the road ahead had been clear, with the exception of the car, and both also confirmed that they had undoubtedly seen the dog, not wandering around or in the side of the road, but suddenly appearing out of the blue in front of the passenger side of the car. It had seemed to bound straight towards the lady, leaving her partner no time to brake safely.

They say the dog was the biggest they had ever seen, a huge Irish wolfhound that looked more the size of a Shetland pony. They also both agreed that even after swerving, there was really no way they could have avoided hitting the dog, and the other puzzling question was what had happened to the car coming in the opposite direction? As it was just passing when the lady's partner swerved into the middle of the road. it seemed to them inevitable that they would hit the other car as well. But this never happened.

The lady's partner says he instinctively looked in his rear view mirror to see what had happened to the other car but he could see nothing, not even the red glow of the rear lights from it. It was as though the car had just disappeared as well.

The lady says she feels as though two periods in time had come together, where the dog seemed to pass through their car before disappearing back to where it had come from, and the other car just seemed to disappear as well as it passed by theirs.

She says that to this day they struggle to make sense of what happened that night, but her partner, who is very sceptical of such things, has had to admit himself that something very strange happened that night, as he can find no logical explanation for the incident. He has also had to agree that if the dog had been flesh and blood there would have undoubtedly been a major accident that night, the consequences of which neither of them like to think about.

Ironbridge Ferry

Only the China Museum remains today to bring back memories of the famous old Coalport China Works that once stood on the riverbanks, producing the famous china that was admired across the world and provided a good living to many of the locals who were employed there.

In those days, a ferry was needed for the residents on the opposite side of the river and a cable-type linkage was used to pull the ferry and its passengers from one side of the Severn to the other. Unfortunately in 1799 during very bad weather conditions, the ferry was damaged and the ferry boat turned over.

Rumour has it that this may have been due to the ferryman playing about, causing the boat itself to tilt from one side to the other and warning his passengers that they might be in for an unplanned swim that day, and, due to this, it accidentally capsized. Reports suggest that up to thirty people lost their lives that day, most of them Coalport China employees, and that some bodies were swept in the fast-moving Severn current as far as Worcester before they were recovered.

Many years later, a young lady was walking along the riverside in the company of other family members. She suddenly stopped, pointing to the water and screamed that she could see a barge on the river and that men and women were shouting and waving their arms about. The other family members looked to where she was pointing, but in a moment everything had vanished and only the girl had really seen those people. From that day forward, people of a sensitive nature have seen visions there and one can only think it must be a relay and haunting of the ghosts of that awful day in 1799 when the ferry sank.

In the 1980s, some unusual pictures were captured by a local amateur photographer which seemed to show people on a similar riverboat ferry appearing to be dancing and waving their arms about, but could this have more likely been their terrible cries for help? Who can say? Was this a haunted shade of a watery crossing to the other side from yesteryear? It could be so.

Ironbridge

My good friend, the late Barry Roberts, told me a most interesting story from a lady who had worked at Coalbrookdale during the Second World War. She had passed on her story to her nephew, Ron, and it was a tale that would be well collaborated by other people later on in life.

Ghost Ferry, Ironbridge.

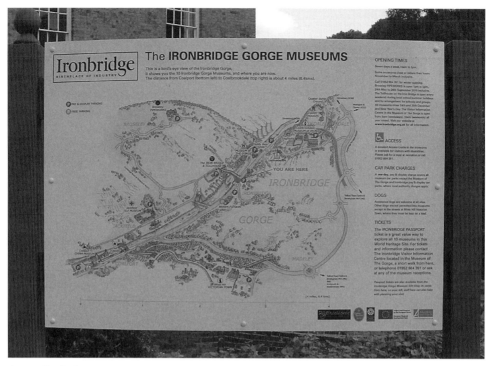

A map of Ironbridge.

The Coalport China Works had closed for the last time in 1926 with the loss of hundreds of jobs locally. Charles Clark Brough had been the director of the works, and often threatened the workers that if a strike ever took place during his time then that would be the end of their employment once and for all. The workers did not heed the warning and did strike.

By this time Charles Clark Brough was not in the best of health and, true to his threats, he shut the works down and moved to a new operation for Coalport in Stoke on Trent. However, it is said that the quality of china produced was not at that time either to his required standards or produced in the way he thought it should be, and Brough ultimately returned to live in a property in nearby Bridgnorth.

As part of the Second World War effort, the old Coalport China Works was turned into a production factory and the house that Brough had actually lived in was used as a canteen for the workers at that time. Brough passed away in 1944; coincidentally, at that time the Luftwaffe's bombing blitz of London was starting to recede somewhat and the couple who had run the canteen announced their intention to return to London, which they did.

They had been very popular with the workers and management and a great effort was made to keep them in post. Allegedly, the couple decided to go south, claiming that the ghost or spirit of an elderly man kept visiting them late at night, spookily looking into individual rooms, including the bedrooms. What was particularly fascinating to many locals was the description the London couple gave of their ghostly visitor, which fitted Mr Charles Brough to a T.

It was also claimed that when Mr Brough returned home from his work at the factory, he would always find it difficult to know which room his wife was in, in the large sprawling house, and would often go from room to room, particularly the bedrooms, searching for her. It would seem that this has continued after his passing to the other side, and there may well be a case for believing that this could have been the spirit of Charles Clark Brough, one time director of the Coalport China Works.

Ironbridge Power Station

A very unusual ghostly apparition was reported by a couple who lived near the power station around 1965. The husband was a night-shift worker and this required his wife to spend nights alone. The Ironbridge of the mid-1960s still had very poor lighting, and the rooms in the little semi-detached house could be extremely dark. No wonder the lady of the house, who was also heavily pregnant at the time, described the building as being a little unnerving at times.

Due to her confinement, she needed to sleep on her back. One evening in the middle of the night she found herself awoken by noises in the room and clearly saw, standing at the bottom of her bed, what she described as a very handsome young man with dark hair and moustache; he was smiling. He was also dressed in an RAF uniform with several medals emblazoned across his chest. With an increased air of intent, he glanced back and nodded. The lady in question said she was not at all afraid and wondered, upon waking the following morning, if she had only been dreaming, but the clarity of her experience made her believe that this was probably not the case.

Shortly after her experience, the lady was putting out her washing on the line when she caught sight of a neighbour whose property adjoined hers at the bottom of the garden. The ladies developed a friendship and one day, whilst sitting in her neighbour's kitchen, she noticed several ornaments and also a glass case with many different objects in it – including an old photograph.

Peering at the picture she could not believe her eyes for a moment, for she felt she recognised the man in it. When her friend returned she did her best to act naturally but asked the question, 'Is it your husband in that photograph?' The neighbour informed her that it wasn't but was in fact her father-in-law who had passed away from a heart attack in his late forties and had for a time lived with the family in the house that she was now living in.

A few days later in her own home, the lady who had had the experience thought she could smell cigarettes burning, but as neither she nor her husband smoked, she couldn't understand this. At other times she was concerned that there may be something on fire in the bathroom. Enquiring again of her friend, she was told that her father-in-law was a heavy smoker.

As time went by, and it was time for the lady to go into hospital to have her baby, there were some difficulties, and the medical staff were very concerned about her well-being. At one stage, as she seemed to be losing consciousness, she heard a medic saying they were going to lose her. But she was not alarmed in any way and felt prepared to let life slip away if that was to be the case. All of a sudden she heard a voice very clearly in her ear saying that she must hold on. She felt quite certain that it was the voice of the ghost she had seen at her home. He continued to say over and over, 'You must listen to the doctors and nurses and concentrate on what they tell you to do.'

Slowly, but surely, she came through her difficulties and things worked out well for her – and she was actually very sad when the time came to leave that little house and the ghost who had proved to be a good friend. Not only did this good spirit serve his country but he helped this lady too, and it's not such an unusual experience as you may imagine, as other people have reported similar experiences to the one this lady had in Ironbridge in the mid-1960s.

The Tontine Hotel, Ironbridge

The bridge itself has its fair share of ghosts, such as the Hooded Monk, the Victorian couple and the two little girls that skip playfully across it. But it is at the Tontine Hotel where one of the most scary stories is told by those that visit or have lived within the building.

This most famous ghostly tale revolves around Room Five, and is said to relate to the murder of Janet, who had been the licensee at the Queen's Head at Ketley. Fredrick, as he is known (and one of the last men to swing by the hangman's noose in Shropshire), is said to have stayed in Room Five before the police captured him for her murder.

To this day, people who stay in Room Five have reported feeling uneasy or have asked to be moved to another room. Clocks chime at unusual hours, the fingers on them have run backwards, and many people have asked the staff about various characters, who can only be described as people of yesteryear, wondering what they are doing in the building. Of course, no one can answer their questions about these people, except to say, 'Oh, it must be our ghosts that you've seen!'

Perhaps one of the most amazing ghost stories I have ever been told happened to a young couple who were from Wolverhampton in the West Midlands but visiting Ironbridge one late Sunday afternoon. The couple had spent a large part of the evening in the nearby Tontine Hotel, which has a long history of hauntings itself but was not on this occasion the source of their experience. By about nine o'clock that night they decided they would have a walk to the other side of the river, which required them to cross the nearby bridge.

Earlier in the day they had bought a small teddy bear from one of the shops, which they intended to give their niece as a present at a later time. As they proceeded to make their way across the bridge, it had become quite dark and they were very startled to see a small black boy running across the bridge towards them, stumbling a little as he came. Stopping him, they asked if he was alright and where he was going, but he just looked at them very vacantly, pointed to the teddy bear in the lady's hand and then pointed to his foot. The couple were horrified to notice that the toes of his right foot appeared to be missing and that he was strangely dressed in clothing of another time. He seemed to reach out and make a grab for the teddy bear; the lady, in what I suppose would be a natural reaction, pulled back her hand to stop him taking it. At that very instant he vanished before their eyes. The lady felt terribly upset and sad and, it has to be said, understandably very scared by the experience too. They were also rather embarrassed that no one believed the experience they'd had, but they were both adamant that it did happen.

Eventually they plucked up the courage to make some enquiries and were told that

Tontine Hotel, Ironbridge.

theirs was not the first story to be told of the boy, and that at one time he had been in the ownership of wealthy local landowners who had treated him very well as a small boy. Yet, when he had got a little older, they decided he would be sent overseas to work for cousins in the New World. Gathering wind of his future to come. The little boy was said to have tried to run away and to have been given the punishment by one of the employees of the landed gentry of having his toes cut off – which unfortunately led to him bleeding to death and although escaping transportation to the Americas, he left this life behind him.

This is certainly the sort of experience that could create a replay of a haunting, but I would say that as the boy had given eye contact to the couple, this was more likely to have been a spirit visitation that was drawn to the young couple rather than a ghost. The gentleman concerned is himself of an afro-Caribbean background, and the couple today are married and settled in the West Midlands. Did the poor little black boy run to them in the hope of being helped and supported? It's a possibility, isn't it?

To this day the couple say they sense this poor little chap was drawn to them, the lady's only really bad feelings about this experience is that she wished she had given the teddy bear to him rather than pull her hand away. A kind thought indeed from this world to a child from the other side, and one can only wonder if other couples similar to them have

The author relaxing at the Tontine Hotel, Ironbridge.

had the same experience. I'm sure that in the right situation and build up of energy it is a possibility that they could do.

The Old Rodney Pub, Ironbridge

Sharon and John had a very strange experience one Christmas Eve, while walking past the Old Rodney pub in Ironbridge. Well, Sharon did at least. It had been snowing quite heavily and there are some steps that go up the side of the building to where the pub is. Sharon says she saw a lady in what she described as a green crinoline dress coming down the steps and appearing to stumble, before vanishing before her very eyes.

John insisted he had seen nothing and suggested that maybe she had had a little too much to drink that evening. Sharon insists she had not and that she had seen a ghost or spirit that would not have come from behind the bar. Old regulars told Sharon that they had heard that once someone had been injured in the area, but they didn't think the description she gave would have fitted in with the tale that they knew. Perhaps she saw something from a time before these particular steps had been built. Who can really say for sure?

Ironbridge

Lee Kind, from Ironbridge, who is a commercial development manager for

The Old Rodney pub at Ironbridge, see steps. (Courtesy of Richard Foxcroft)

Tarmac National Contracting, said he saw a scary sight during a drive in heavy fog. He says, 'I actually drove through a man, a woman and two children who were standing, not floating, just standing in my lane, holding hands. To this day, and every time I think of them, I get a shudder down my spine and wonder who they were and why they were there.'

This is a particularly interesting story, because in my experience as an investigator of the paranormal, many drivers, especially people such as long-distance lorry drivers and drivers of agricultural vehicles, who tend to drive at unusual hours and in all conditions, often have the same sort of experiences that Lee had.

Of course, this sort of thing also happens to other people, but luckily when they stop their vehicle they always find there is nothing there, and can only come to the conclusion that it must have been a ghostly spectre that their vehicle has travelled through, and perhaps a replay of another time.

But this must be one of the most scary and frightening experiences one could possibly have and, as Lee put it, would certainly put a shudder down your spine and mine, if we had a similar experience; of that I'm sure!

The Boat Inn, Jackfield

It is at the Boat Inn that some have claimed that a game of cards was played between an unsuspecting miner and the Devil himself. Anything is possible, and to this day people say they hear the sound of hoof-like tapping on one particular table. Windows that open on their own and the sobbing of a young woman have also been reported in the past at the inn.

Mary told me a very interesting story. Many years ago when she was walking past the building with her friend, she saw an unusual creature that looked rather like a goat. It was a foggy evening and Mary and her friend were scared by what they saw. Of course, it is a possibility that it was just a goat, and in the mist they couldn't see if it was accompanied by someone or had just got loose. The girls were quite prepared to accept this as a possibility at the time, but Mary, even to this day, is quite convinced that it was of another world and an evil entity at that. Who knows, she may be right!

The Red Church, Jackfield

The old Red Church now has very little left to show for its finery of yesteryear. Apparently, it was Lady Blythe who financed the building of the Red Church by leaving a substantial amount of money for its erection and maintenance. Legend has it that she also gave specific instructions as to where it was to be built.

However, it seems that those who built the church decided her choice of location at the top of the hill was a bad one and it would be much better built at the bottom of the hill. We are told that foundations that were laid at the bottom would be mysteriously removed from their setting and placed at the top of the hill during the hours of darkness, and it would seem that Lady Blythe brought some influence from the other side, because it was eventually built at the top of the hill!

Unfortunately, only the trace foundations, and some gravestones which were erected in a corner of a small field as the burial ground, are worthy of a visit today. However, another ghost story revolves around the place where it is claimed that during the cholera epidemic, when the church was still standing, at night the ghost of a woman in frock, bonnet and long coat was seen swinging a lantern to and fro and calling, 'Bring out your dead!'

Jackfield rooftops. (Courtesy of Richard Foxcroft)

At one time a footpath between Jackfield and Broseley is also where people would find their path obstructed by some sort of force of energy or supernatural blockage, strong enough to force people to go back and find their way home by a different route. Some believe this is the ghost of a mother and daughter, known as Elizabeth and the little pathway lass and, furthermore, that the little girl may have been murdered by a male friend of Elizabeth and searches forever more, only really wanting to know if passers by can tell her where her mother is. A very sad, but one has to say, very scary ghost story.

Jiggers Bank

The local postman had a very scary experience while delivering the mail one morning some years ago. Making his way through Horsehay and onto the top of Jiggers Bank in his van, a mist suddenly developed in front of him, and within it a man's face formed. Swerving to avoid collision and braking fiercely, he still felt quite sure he must have injured someone, but no one was to be seen. The strange thing was, the electrical system on his vehicle then completely failed and refused to start again.

Legend has it that this may have something to do with an incident many years ago, when a young Telford lad who worked on a nearby farm was courting a young servant girl whounfortunately, brought their relationship to an abrupt end. Unable to continue with his life, it is said the young man drowned himself in Horsehay pool but occasionally returns to this world looking for his long-lost love.

Maureen and Peter, as a courting couple in the 1970s, had an unusual experience in this area too. As they walked hand in hand, suddenly all around them they had the sense of a male and female voice arguing, but nothing was to be seen. The couple say it continued for quite a few seconds and then they heard the sound of crying and a man pleading for forgiveness. Maybe the couple had what is called a clairaudient experience; this is where you can hear or link into experiences with relation to spirits or ghosts but not see them, and it may well be that this was also the ghostly energy that drained the energy of the postman's van. It is a distinct possibility, isn't it?

The White Lion Pub, Ketley

Debbie and Andrew run the White Lion pub, which was built in 1661 and was an old coaching inn. It is on the old London to Holyhead Road and Dick Turpin is alleged to have stopped there on his travels.

Their resident ghost is referred to as Charlie, although they are not sure why, as he was known of and already called that before they moved into the premises. He is certainly active, though, and switches the television on full-blast in one of the upstairs bedrooms; this comes on at all hours of the night when no one is in the room. He also turns the stop-tap off in the gents' toilets and the gas tap off in the cellar.

Also, in the early hours of the morning, the hand-dryer in the ladies' toilets is often switched on and can be heard, although there is definitely no one in there at the time. It would seem that perhaps Charlie is fascinated with the gadgets from the modern world and loves to fiddle around with the buttons, switches, taps, and so on, in the building.

Pictures also drop off the walls occasionally for no apparent reason and footsteps are regularly heard running across the landing when there is no one upstairs. This has been heard by more than one person on numerous occasions in the downstairs rooms.

Ketley Brook

Some years ago, a group of young men were out early in the morning poaching for rabbits by setting snares and laying nets, when suddenly they heard the sound of twigs breaking as someone approached them. Setting their lamps on the figure that appeared in front of them, they saw a very large old-fashioned policeman with truncheon drawn and whistle in mouth.

Legend has it that at one time in this area a young bobby had been shot by poachers. Was the young officer still doing his duty in the Ketley Brook area? The poachers didn't stop to find out, and I shouldn't think many others who follow this practice, would tend to report such an incident if they had a similar experience, would they? So who knows how many others have seen this vision!

The White Lion, Ketley.

Lawley Bank

Mavis Price wrote to me to say she has experienced many psychic, ghostly and paranormal events for many years. In the 1980s at the premises where she worked, which is now a local community centre in Telford, a member of staff told her she had heard someone on the stairs, although the doors were locked and she was alone with her husband. Her husband, who could also hear the footsteps, checked the premises but couldn't find anything that could have caused them.

Mavis mentioned this to one of the local community policemen and also told him about one of the doors that kept opening by itself. He laughed, saying they mustn't have shut the door securely, so he was invited to try it for himself. He slammed the door closed and then sat by it to see what would happen. When the door opened by itself in front of him, he dashed into the room to check if there was anyone inside. It was empty and he had to admit that there had to be 'someone else there'! Mavis says that while she was attending a meeting one evening at the building, the door opened again, footsteps were heard, and then the outer door opened and closed. Another person who witnessed this asked if this was their ghost – Mavis replied that indeed it was.

She also says that in the late 1970s, she had moved to a new house with her husband and daughter in the Lawley Bank area. One night, her daughter said someone kept following her from the front door to the kitchen and had poked her in the back. Another time she saw the outline of a figure. A few weeks after this, Mavis says she saw a shadowy figure and felt someone sit at the end of her bed. They got used to these things happening and, for some reason, started to call the ghost Ashley. She says that when something unexplainable happened, they used to say, 'Hello Ashley.'

They tried to find out a bit more about the occurrences and went to see a medium, who mentioned the ghost, saying he was friendly and also had his wife with him, but they couldn't understand why Mavis and her family were on their premises. Sometime later, Mavis was talking to an elderly man from the housing estate they lived on, who told her some things about the area. He said that the land where their house was used to belong to a farmer who, unfortunately, had been killed by one of his bulls. *The farmer's name was Mr Ashley!*

Mavis says strange occurrences have also taken place in the local pub, called the Arleston Inn, where she and some friends take part in quizzes and the like every week and she even felt someone touch her leg on one occasion. Very spooky indeed. She says that her grandson has also had various experiences of 'seeing' people from a very young age and that one day his mother saw him waving out of the window. When she asked who he was waving to, he said the old

58

lady in the garden. His mother says there was no old lady there. On another occasion when he couldn't sleep he climbed into bed with his mother. She saw the bedroom door move and he said, 'It's only Grandad.' He was then able to settle down to sleep.

Another incident was when he was playing football in the garden and saw his grandad waving to him from his car. He waved back and, when his mother asked him who he was waving to, on this occasion he told her, 'It's only Grandad going to the pub for a pint.' Each time these things occurred, Mavis says her daughter could see no one at all.

Lilleshall

Steve emailed me saying that he used to work at Lilleshall National Sports Centre, which is based on what was the Duke of Sutherland's Hunting Lodge that was built in 1831, a very solid building in white stone. Steve says that according to other staff members, there are several ghosts in the building, but the following are the experiences he and his son had while they were there.

They worked in the maintenance department and one of their duties was to annually clean the many oil-fired boilers, three of which are situated in the basement of the main house. Steve's son was cleaning the middle boiler of the row of three, when he felt a presence in the room. He looked up from his crouched position and saw a man wearing a dark blue trilby hat and sitting in the corner of the room watching him.

The son quickly realised that the man was not of this earth, and, becoming alarmed, fled out of the room, ran up the stairs and out into the forecourt, and then to the boss's office. The boss asked him what the apparition looked like, and as he

reached the bit '...wearing a blue trilby hat,' his words were echoed by another member of the maintenance department, an old hand who had worked there many years, who, although never having admitted to seeing a ghost, had heard of this one from other people.

After dinner, he got his nerve up and returned to his task in the boiler room. At tea-time he met Steve in the tea room and told his father that there had been another ghost sitting in the opposite corner of the boiler room. This one was a man wearing spectacles and a boiler suit, and was rocking back and forth. This time the son ignored him, but the apparition remained there for several minutes.

The following day, Steve went to the boiler room to do the daily routine checks on the plant. He noticed that the Yale cylinder lock on the door had worked loose, and on completing all plant room checks he returned to fix the lock. As he was working on the lock he caught a flash of light at the opposite end of the room. Turning, he saw the apparition of the man in specs as described by his son; he was rocking as if in a rocking chair. He was halfway into a wall, which was a later addition to the room to contain the oil tank. Apparently the room had always been a boiler room but was originally coal-fired. As he rocked, his head was moving in and out of the light from a large ventilation grille and the light was reflecting off his spectacles. Steve says he could see right through him as if he was made of water, although, to his son, he was as solid as a real person, as was the other ghost he saw.

As Steve continued repairing the lock, which took about five minutes, he kept glancing back at the apparition which remained there, still rocking. Summoning up his courage, he walked towards the vision, approaching to within about 4ft, where it

Romany people are superstitious, as the author well knows

was still clearly visible. At this point Steve began to feel a chill around him and, finally losing his nerve, left the room very briskly.

One night Steve had to supervise some contractors who were working on the water tank in King's Hall, a gymnasium. They decided to start work late in the evening so as not to disrupt people's use of the facilities. They finished the job at around 3 a.m. and he helped by walking down the long corridor where all the shower rooms were, turning on the cold taps to vent the air. There are two fire doors in the corridor and as he approached the first one, he could hear the laughter of children and the faint sound of running feet. Turning and looking behind him, he saw two little girls and a little boy run past him and through the closed door. Looking through the glass panel in the door about 3ft away, he could see them veer to the right and disappear through the solid brick wall. Steve says they were barely visible to him and he could see right through them.

He consulted his friend, the old hand, who said he hadn't heard of this occurrence before. The man said he believed the place had been a Dr Barnardo's Home at some time in the past. It seemed to Steve that the children came from a time before the Hall was built and he wonders if the fact that the whole of the area is made up of naturally occurring sandstone, which contains iron, acts as a recorder for these events to be seen by the human eye. Perhaps it was something pleasant that had happened, arousing strong emotions in the children, causing this to be recorded in the ether.

On another evening, he had just picked his wife up from work when he had a call asking him if he could attend to a fault. He left his wife in the tea room, and on returning she told him there was a ghost sitting in there with her. When he told his co-workers the following day, they told him his wife's description of the ghost matched that of the old boss who had died a couple of years earlier.

Another time when he had taken his wife into the old house through the main entrance, which is quite grand with a short flight of steps down inside the ante-room, she saw someone wearing a flat cloth cap and a boiler suit standing at the top of the steps. Steve says that his wife's grandmother was a Romany gypsy and feels that this might have some bearing on his wife and son seeing all sorts of supernatural occurrences.

Steve says his boss told him that after attending a New Year's party in the old house, he took a room there for the night after the party had gone on until past midnight and some! He was just getting into bed when he heard the sound of a hunting horn. Looking out of the windows nothing could be seen, despite some outdoor lighting. He enquired of a friend in another nearby room, suspecting a prank; his friend told him he had done no such thing and had not heard anything either. When he asked around the other guests the following morning, he also drew a blank.

Various staff members told Steve some other spooky tales; one was that there was the ghost of an old housekeeper that walked the upper corridors of the old house and was of fearsome countenance. Someone else who was a member of the maintenance department told him of when they had a job to do on the first floor of the old house and, with arms full of tools,

went up the back stairs. At the top of the stairs there is a landing leading to a double door and he was somewhat chagrined to find the doors closed; there had been a fire alarm check during which all the doors in the corridors automatically close.

As he got to the doors, preparing to put all his tools down to open them, they seemingly opened of their own accord and latched back onto their magnetic catches. As there was absolutely no one in sight who could have done this, he quickly gathered all his tools together and flew back down the stairs, saying he would never go into the old house on his own again. Presumably, he may have had an encounter with one of the previous boiler-house occupants!

Steve's friend, the old hand, mentioned earlier, related this following story to him. The rooms upstairs were used for offices, and one day the ladies occupying one of those rooms called maintenance because they said they were feeling cold. He went to check the radiator, which he found quite warm to the touch, but he turned it up to maximum.

Later that day he was called back to the room as it was still very cold. He checked the windows for draughts and found none. He then removed the thermostat from the radiator valve, allowing it to be fully open. He said he couldn't keep his hand on the radiator for even a few seconds as it was so hot, but having checked the temperature with an electronic thermometer, which was regularly calibrated, strangely, it was reading zero. He said the room inexplicably remained in this state for five days and nights with the ladies having to work with their coats on, according to his account.

The Duke of Sutherland had a private office which is situated over the offshoot entrance to the house. The room is split-level, the first part having a low ceiling, the second outer part having a high ceiling. The duke decided to have a balcony erected there, the floor of which is level with the bottom of the windows and a staircase with ornate newels gives access to it. It is said that he would sit up there keeping an eye on the estate workers, and was quick to punish any he thought were slacking.

A maid called Mary was allegedly found dead hanging from the upper newel post. One version of this story says she was sitting in the duke's chair, and upon spotting him riding through the forecourt gateway, she went to run from the room, but caught her apron strap on the newel post, causing her body to swing over the rail. The second version says that having been discovered to be pregnant, she was dismissed from her job and accommodation and that she hung herself from the newel post. Whether the duke was responsible for the poor girl's state is unknown.

Steve says that this particular room often felt abnormally cool at times when he entered it during monthly emergency light testing. Also, when they entered the room to replace the reflectors in the office-type neon strip lights, which had been used previously as an office and then changed back to accommodation, they would be hanging out of the light fittings by their safety strings. He also says that although one light fitting could have been reached by an occupant standing on a chair, the other one at the high end of the room needed a step ladder to reach it.

Steve very sensibly points out that some of the stories he was told and has heard about may have just been hearsay, but they are very interesting and in my opinion very supportive of the overall experiences Steve, his wife and son had there – well worthy of inclusion in the annals of *Haunted Telford*.

Leegomery

There was an unusual copse in Leegomery at one time which no longer exists, just over the canal bridge travelling towards Haughton, and was an area where children used to play. It was here that local youngsters in the past often reported the sound of footsteps or running, from no physical source, and also the appearance of a young girl who seemed to have no feet and no visual face and was said to simply float by. The dress she was wearing was described as being from the Victorian period and some have also spoken of the sweet smell of lavender as the young lady, known by some as Little Sarah, passes by. She is described as face-less, but apparently not frightening, in the words of some witnesses.

Madeley

This town has more than its share of strange goings-on: a spectre that strides through the town known as the Laughing Cavalier, the Green Lady or Matilda, who has been known to smile sweetly and speak to those sensitive to such things with a pleasant, 'Good evening, Sir,' or 'Good evening, Madam,' which of course means this must be a spirit rather than a ghost.

A lot of people say to me that surely a ghost and spirit are the same thing, but they most certainly are not. A ghost is generally only a replay over and over of something that has happened in the past, perhaps something bad or occasionally something quite pleasant, and can be sensed or witnessed, whereas a spirit is the part of all of us that continues and goes on forever.

A good way of knowing the difference between a ghost and spirit is that generally a ghost will not acknowledge you or communicate with you – it just walks past and perhaps vanishes, but a spirit has the ability to communicate and interact with you if it wishes, and that is the difference in simple terms.

Witchcraft in Madeley

There are some well-known witchcraft stories in Telford which include the following two stories. In one a horse, and in the other a calf, are cursed by a witch. When the witch in each case was threatened with violence, they very quickly responded by saying, 'May God bless you and your beast'. It could be that their god was Wiccan or perhaps one of the old pagan gods, but the agricultural people of the time felt quite sure that the 'witches' meant Satan himself.

Towards the end of the nineteenth century, a most impressive account and report of Shropshire's folklore was presented in an excellent tome by Charlotte Burne and Georgina Jackson. But one old Salopian who spoke to Charlotte Burne rejected the whole idea of ghosts, spirits and paranormal possibilities in good old-fashioned Salop dialect of the day, saying, 'I dunna believe as there's owt in it as the dead come back, and if they bin to t'other place, they would'na be let to!' I think this is quite an interesting little item for readers of this book today and a very good example of the way people of this area spoke in the past.

However, it has to be said that many of the older folk did believe in ghosts and spirits and told stories that have been passed down to us to this day, and most certainly would not say, 'I dunna believe there's owt in it!'

Madeley

One of the region's most unusual ghost stories is animalistic in nature and concerns the Roaring Bull that was said to represent the ghost of an evil squire and it has been seen in many areas, but particularly Madeley and the land that today is the site of the famous Blists Hill Museum. Legend has it that the entity was captured in a bottle. Catching a ghost in a box or a bottle was commonly reported in tales of old Telford and Shropshire in times gone by.

Madeley Churchyard

This is where a man, making an early morning visit, saw a figure at the bottom of the slope. He felt this was unusual as dawn was only just breaking. Bravely moving down the slope to satisfy his curiosity, he saw that two fresh graves were dug out and covered over ready for funerals that he assumed were to take place later that day.

Seeing a small old lady standing by the graves, he started to walk over towards her to see if she was alright. However, in the twinkling of an eye she dissolved before his very eyes. One can only assume that this was either a visitation from a spirit or

The author at St Michael's churchyard, Madeley.

a ghost, perhaps paying respects to the dead or maybe even waiting for a loved one to join her and paying her last respects before that reunion took place.

The Creatures of Madeley Court

The old courthouse at Madeley was lived in by the abbots of Wenlock before the Dissolution. Unusual visions have been seen and reported in this area on a regular basis throughout history. These include an old lady who wears a long black skirt with a hood pulled up over her head. There is also the legend of Romanies or gypsies appearing in and around the building; some people hypothesise the view that they were ill-treated at some time and the visitation is relevant to a curse being placed on some local residents.

Perhaps even more bone-chilling is the story of creatures described as neither man nor beast that once followed a teenager and so unnerved him that he was never comfortable walking past the windmill area there in future years. In more recent times, two teenage girls described two dark shapes that seemed to be breathing very heavily just behind them and they were very scared by their experience. Could this be the experience of shape-shifting? Or could it be as the girls described, the monsters of Madeley?

The Monks of Madeley Court

Marcus told me a most interesting story concerning the building. He was led to believe that the hotel had been a monastery many hundreds of years ago and that a number of unpleasant events had happened to the monks by order of a ruthless king, or possibly lord, who wanted the monasteries and land for himself. Legend has it that the monks were murdered but still return and roam around the grounds to this day, appearing to be chanting or perhaps meditating. He also spoke of a particular oak panel in one of the reading rooms where a face of one of the original monks peers out.

Perhaps even more spooky is the story of taxi drivers that have been called who, eventually arriving at the building, found it difficult to find as strange mists have built up before them. Other drivers tell of the strange experience of being greeted by a man who says they are required to go to the reception desk and wait there, who they later find is not part of the staff and some claim is apparently not of this world – not the present time at least! There are many other stories associated with the Madeley Court Hotel, but perhaps this is one of the most fascinating ones I was told and is very spooky indeed.

Madeley Wood

Many people throughout the world have told the story of visions of Sasquatch, the native American word for a huge ape-like man, Bigfoot, the Abominable Snowman, and so on. Telford also has its story of such a monkey-man.

One comes from the Fortean expert and author, Mike Dash. While researching

Philip Solomon at the Court House Mill, Madeley. The building is adjacent to Madeley Court Hotel.

Court House Green Room, Madeley.

Court House, Madeley.

the subject area, Dash came across a copy of the 1878 edition of *Sheldrake's Aldershot and Sandhurst Military Gazette* with a most interesting Telford story linked to it. It claimed that for a fortnight around the Madeley Wood area of Salop, efforts had been made to capture a gorilla-type animal said to be appearing around the vicinity. It appears that some people believed the sightings were relevant to a huge monkey that had escaped from a travelling circus or something similar on its way to Bridgnorth. Excellent authoritative witnesses came forward, including a local policeman and clergyman, who both perhaps rather sensibly quickly fled the scene! Who wouldn't in the pitch darkness?

One occupier of a house in Madeley Wood also reports having had a terrifying experience. She had visited friends in the evening as the rest of her family had gone to bed. As was often the case in Madeley in those times, she had left the front door unlocked. Upon returning home, she was horrified at seeing a bent form with a very hairy face crouching over the fire, apparently warming itself in the dark.

Too frightened to scream, she ran to her neighbours, who armed themselves with guns, pitchforks and other paraphernalia ready to defend themselves from what they believed to be a huge ape-type creature. Entering her home, there indeed was the huge, horrific figure now sitting in a chair by the fire. Roused and alarmed by the group, it rose to its full height and was clearly the figure of a well-known character known as Old Johnny, who, finding the door unlocked, had walked in and was enjoying the warmth of the fire and smoking the master's pipe.

It is a funny story I know, but other rumours have suggested there is more to this than just a humorous story and possibly the truth was hushed up. It is a fact that the animal was never found and other stories of such ape-like creatures abound in Telford and nearby Shropshire generally.

Nick Redfern has written extensively of the so-called man-monkey of Bridge 39 on the Shropshire Union Canal, apparently in reference to Charlotte S. Burne and Georgina F. Jackson's book, *Shropshire Folklore*, which tells of an unusual encounter with a so-called animal ghost in 1879. An agricultural carter was employed to take luggage from Ranton in Staffordshire to Woodcock near Newport in Shropshire. Around 10 p.m. that evening, the horse being very tired and labouring, could only move very slowly, and arriving at a bridge that crosses the Birmingham & Liverpool Canal, faltered.

Just before crossing the bridge, a huge black creature with great glowing eyes jumped out of the hedge and leapt onto the horse's back. The carter tried to frighten it off with his whip, but as he cracked the whip across its back, it simply went through the creature and landed on the ground. The horse was very tired but in its terror immediately flew into a gallop and crossed the bridge at full speed with the ghost-monkey still on its back, before the creature simply vanished into thin air. The carter hurried to the nearby village of Woodseaves and although petrified told the full story to all who would listen. This is the basis of Nick Redfern's *Story of the Man Monkey*, an excellent read for anyone wishing to know more of this story.

But other people have also told stories of seeing a similar creature in wooded areas and by canals. Do they all relate back to the original story of the ape-like creature that was seen in Madeley Wood? The American-Indian tribes accept there is such a creature that comes from another world and can appear and disappear at will – a Sasquatch, but I suppose those of us in places such as Telford and Shropshire would consider it to be, if not real, then paranormal and in that context, basically what one could only describe as a ghost.

The Saintly Girl of Much Wenlock

There are many stories linked to a beautiful girl described as a saint. The story goes that she was pursued by an amorous young man with ill-intent in mind. Whilst riding one day and being chased by the lusty man, she fell from her horse and was killed. Legend has it that she takes pity on any poor maid in trouble and brings help and peace to them.

Karen told me a very interesting story about one night when she was walking through the town after saying goodnight to her boyfriend. She felt quite sure a man was following her. Looking round he seemed to stop and look away, but as she walked on and quickened her step, she heard his footsteps do the same behind her. In her own words, she was absolutely terrified and felt quite sure that this man had evil intentions and that an attack on her was most likely.

Walking very quickly round a corner, she saw before her what she described as an angel, or a lady that glowed. She just felt drawn to run as fast as she could from that moment on and didn't stop until she got home and felt that the man who had been following her had been stopped from doing so. Could this have been the ghost or spirit of the beautiful girl that people had described as saintly? It is certainly quite an amazing story.

There are also numerous other ghosts, including those that are described as tall monks that step out in front of cars. People have also reported time-slip experiences, thinking for a moment they are in another time in history and, if driving, usually accompanied with strange experiences of engines cutting out for no apparent reason. This seems to happen particularly around November.

Much Wenlock

Not all ghost stories are old ones and this one from the local supermarket falls into the newer category. But there is believed to be a historical link to it. Just a few years ago, a lot of improvements and building alterations were being made to the Spar supermarket, which is just off the main square in Much Wenlock itself.

As the work started up, lots of strange things started to happen. The sound of heavy breathing was heard and various spectres and apparitions were seen by customers and staff alike. Many people believed this problem had been created because of the ground being disturbed during building excavation, where the builders, while digging there, had found old bones and some unusual pottery under the building.

Things got to such a state that it was brought to the attention of BBC Midlands *Today,* who became interested in the proceedings and reported on this particular haunting. A trainee manager reported that, while at work on the computer, hard, heavy breathing was heard but no one was ever there. Trolleys stacked in the storeroom area would inexplicably move about of their own accord and another member of staff experienced the feeling of a hand being placed on their shoulder. The store supervisor, Mr Anderson, also reported a very strange experience he had. Popping into the back area of the supermarket, he saw something suddenly appear. It stayed in his vision for a full fifteen to twenty seconds and then simply vanished into thin air.

Some research has suggested that the supermarket may have been built on the site of a very ancient alehouse, but nothing of this sort of business has been found. However, the builders did say that they had found a lot of what they believed to be human bones, together with interesting items of pottery. Further research also suggests that the abbey cemetery may have been in this vicinity in the twelfth century, so perhaps you may get more than you bargained for while shopping at the site of this old building! There again, perhaps someone from another world might be kind enough to push your trolley round for you!

Raynald's Mansion House, Much Wenlock

In the High Street of Much Wenlock not far from the old Corn Exchange, there is a rather plain timber-framed building said to be from the Elizabethan days and called Raynald's Mansion House. It has rather elaborate facades to it and if you look up towards the upper storeys of the building, you can see two doors and porches above. Between the doors there is a bar and post which many years ago was used by staff to lift heavy objects on to their backs for carrying.

Some people say they have seen visions of a man there who appears hunched over and with a grimacing face, others have reported seeing children who they describe as being dressed in Victorian clothes, playing and dancing on the balconies. It would seem that these visions of yesteryear are those of one poor soul preparing for toil, while the children were dancing and playing above him. No wonder this ghostly vision is described as being grim-faced. Wouldn't you be?

Newport

Rachel contacted me with a story of when she moved to a new house in Granville Road, with her two sons. It wasn't until after she had purchased the house that people told her there was something strange about it, and that people who had lived there previously seemed to get divorced or tried to commit suicide, or other various bad things happened to them.

When she moved in, she knew that the previous person who had lived there had had some sort of breakdown and had painted the doors in some weird colours, but she was quite handy with a paintbrush and set to work making the place look the way she wanted it. About a week or so later, odd little things started to occur, like finding the lights on when they came down in the morning, or the radio switched on when it had been switched off before they went to bed.

Other things they found after coming downstairs in the mornings were open cupboard doors that had been shut, the kettle sometimes feeling warm as though it hadn't long been boiled and quite often the distinctive smell of pipe smoke. Doors in the house were open when Rachel was quite sure that they had been shut before retiring for the night, and the children's school bags and toys had often been moved from where they had been left. These things happened quite regularly and for whatever reason, Rachel says she used to comment, 'Oh, George has been here again!'

Not long after this, her younger son, who was about five at the time, told her that when he had gone to the bathroom upstairs he had seen a man on the landing smoking a pipe. Although open-minded about these things, she had made light of it so as not to scare the children. A couple of nights later, something seemed to wake her up in the night and she saw an elderly gentleman dressed in what she described as clothes from another time, such as that of a farmer or blacksmith and wearing what looked like a thick apron.

Her garage, which was adjoined to the property, had a door inside which opened into the house. There was also an up-and-over door which opened onto the front of the house from the garage. One day, after she had stripped a couple of the rooms of wallpaper to redecorate, she had gathered up the rubbish and put it all into bin liners, and then taken them into the garage to put in the boot of the car.

When she got up the next day, the door from the house to the garage was open. She didn't take too much notice at first, as this, along with lots of other things, had become a regular occurrence at the house. But then she discovered the up and over garage door was wide open and it looked as though someone had been in, probably youngsters, who had tried to set fire to the wallpaper and other rubbish. Strangely, though, it hadn't actually caught fire and she says it also looked as though someone had been trying to put it out.

She called the police and someone from the station came round to take notes about what had happened. The police officer said he couldn't understand how the whole lot hadn't gone up in flames and they were very lucky as there were gas pipes, electrical wiring and so on in the garage. If if a fire had reached them it could have caused an explosion that would have affected the whole street, not just their house. Rachel says she feels sure it was 'George' who had intervened to put out the fire.

Rachel says they have since moved to another property, but not because of the things that happened while they were living at the house, as she says she never felt scared and there were no bad feelings there. In fact, she was quite intrigued by it all and said that, out of curiosity, she made some enquiries about the house and the area generally, and found out that on the site where the housing estate called Ashworth Way had been built in the late 1980s, for many years previously, a large wood yard had been there called Ashworth's Timber Yard. She feels that George had something to do with the yard, but says she still has to do some more research to find out just who he was and why he was around the house so much.

The Old Oakengates Railway Track

Bill Taylor told me a very interesting story of when he was a boy and found himself in a place where his friend and he really shouldn't have been, for they had strayed out of curiosity onto the old railway track at Oakengates:

We'd been playing quite happily for about ten minutes when we saw what we believed to be a real man in a long leather coat, swinging an old-fashioned lantern and shouting at us, 'Get out of here you little fools! I know who you are.' Well, we both ran for our lives because in those days doing wrong would bring you punishment from your parents and we knew if he knew our dads we would really be in trouble, so we went home and told our parents what

Old railway station, Oakengates. (Courtesy of Richard Foxcroft)

we had done. We did both get punished, and severely at that and my father then went to the railway people to apologise, but no one could actually say who the old man in the leather coat might have been. To this day I am quite certain my friend and I saw a ghost, so perhaps we got doubly punished for playing on the railway tracks near Oakengates Station that day!

The Haunted Oakengates Piano

Alan told me a very interesting story of a clock that stopped at the very moment that his grandfather died, yet very strangely started up again on the day of his funeral. Apparently, the family were so convinced that it was haunted by the old man that they sold it to some travellers, only later to find out that it was a very valuable timepiece. Was the old chap actually trying to warn

the family of its value? It's not beyond the bounds of possibility, is it? In my many years of investigating the paranormal, this is not the first example I have been told of such experiences either.

Many years ago, I had some friends who lost their mother who had lived on her own for many years. Her pride and joy had been a piano in the front room that she insisted no one could ever touch and, when they were children, she had always warned them never to touch the Old Joanna.

Removal people were called in to do a house clearance and of course the piano went with it. Not that unusual, you might think, but the day before the house clearance, the daughter, while visiting the house to clean up, felt quite sure that she had heard the sound of piano notes being played in the front room. Running in she clearly saw that there was no one there and felt it must have been her imagination.

After the lady's funeral, while in conversation with an uncle that she had not seen for many years, she was rather shocked when he said he hoped they'd looked inside the piano itself, saying, 'You do know your mother always kept £1,000 in there for a rainy day, don't you?' The next day she immediately phoned the dealers who had cleared the property and they invited her to go to examine the piano, but there was nothing to be found.

She never really thought very much about this again and was quite sure it was just a family tale. However, visiting a local theatre some years later to watch a demonstration of mediumship from a well-known medium, she received a message from the stage enquiring if she knew a lady who owned an old black piano from the other side. 'She tells me you should never have got rid of that piano, my dear, it might have been worth a fortune to you one day.'

Coincidence? Well, it could have been, and who can really say for sure? But I suppose this particular Telford lady will always wonder what the truth really was and were those piano notes she heard, trying to tell her that there were pound notes for her in the Old Joanna?

Oakengates Theatre

The Theatre in Limes Walk, Oakengates, has always been a place where strange noises have been heard. One of the old technicians and backroom staff told me that doors would open on their own, windows would be found inexplicably unlocked, and wind blew around the building, and the aroma of lavender would be experienced at quiet times. One lady told me of a strange experience she had while cleaning the stage area; she heard what she described as the sound of a fur coat being dragged across the floor.

There is also a particular seat in the theatre that is described as being spooky, to say the least, but for the benefit of the booking office it is probably as well that I do not tell you which seat it is! But if you have ever visited the theatre and felt terribly cold where you were sitting then now you know why! Icy cold, I am told, is the feeling that is felt upon one's posterior and shoulders and, having sat in this particular seat myself, I have to endorse this view.

I have personally put forward the view that every theatre has its ghosts and shades of yesteryear, for this is exactly the sort of place where excitement, exhilaration and tension would be created and put in place by theatre visitors and, of course, the wonderful people from the acting profession.

A Funeral Procession in Priorslee

Tony and Alison had a very strange experience whilst attending the funeral of an elderly uncle. The gentleman had been very well respected in the town so perhaps it was no surprise to the couple to see an old man, in what appeared to be a field, raise his hat as the funeral cortege passed by. The strange thing was, when asking later at the family wake who this was, they were assured there was no such field in place and no one had seen this happen.

Quite sure of what they had seen, the couple decided to re-drive the route but nothing was to be found. An elderly aunt explained to them that it was a tradition in Telford for the men to 'doff' their cap or hat at any funeral procession, both as a mark of

Oakengates Theatre, Limewalk.

The author entering the Theatre at Oakengates.

respect and to keep away bad luck. Was this an agricultural labourer from another time paying his respects? It seems it may have been.

Priorslee

Steve told me about some of the experiences his wife had when she worked in the Co-op in Priorslee. The shop is built on the site of what was once some farm buildings, and the frontage of the shop and the chemist shop next door appear to be original to the farm. Across the rear of the shops are the stores, office, washroom and toilet. An occurrence that seemed to happen quite often was the girls were unable to open the door to the washroom to get out – the door refused to open until someone actually opened it from the outside. Steve even checked the lock himself and found nothing wrong with it.

One day his wife was in the washroom when the ghost of a woman appeared in there. She seemed to be between fifty-five and sixty years old and was wearing a patterned work overall. She appeared to his wife several times after that in the stores and on the shop floor after closing at ten o'clock at night. On occasion, the large cartons containing cereals that were quite light in weight and stored on the top shelves, would be forcibly flung off the shelves and would hit the opposite wall some 6ft away, in full view of her!

Some of the staff who worked there found an old rusty key somewhere in the stores area one day and it was put to one side in the office by the staff working on the two to ten shift. The following afternoon when his wife went in for the next two to ten shift, she was told that the morning shift staff had found a rusty key on the floor, outside the office which had been securely locked the previous night. So they decided to lock the key in the safe, but, the following day, once more the morning shift staff swore they had found it on the floor outside the office again.

The Spectral Fire of Shifnal

At one time I had family who lived in Madeley and Shifnal. One winter's evening, many years ago, my great aunt who lived in Shifnal passed away and her home was empty for some time. My family who lived in Madeley were short of coal that winter; coal had been in short supply for most people that year.

Two of the family sisters knew very well that their aunt had a good supply of coal that was going to waste, so they made their way to her home with a large shopping bag intending to collect a supply. They were surprised to find, on arriving at the house, that in the little fireplace a fire was already prepared, paper was wrapped in balls with a bit of wood on top of it and a good supply of coal on top of that.

Their aunt was a practical woman and she had obviously prepared the fire which was just waiting to be lit. This made them a little sad, but they went down into the cellar, all in complete darkness by now, and by candlelight they filled the bag with lumps of coal. Coming back up the stairs and into the small front room, they were both aghast to see that the little fire was now ablaze and the whole room was very warm. Even more scary, their aunt's rocking chair was rocking to and fro. The two girls looked at each other, dropped the bag and fled the building.

The next day their father visited the house in question, to check their story. There was the prepared fire as they described, but it had certainly not been

Streets of Shifnal.

alight. What had happened that night can only remain a mystery, but I do know that this is a completely true story.

Naughty Nell's, Shifnal

The Naughty Nell public house is a very haunted place and somewhere I have investigated myself on numerous occasions, leaving me in no doubt that the building is haunted. Figures have been seen of a male publican and serving wenches, and unusual fragrances fill the air – sometimes quite unpleasant, sometimes with the fragrance of lavender or roses.

One character who is known to scare people occasionally is Mr Rudge, who wears a long leather apron and has piercing eyes. At one time, while the old pub was being developed, building workers refused to continue their work until, in their words, an end was put to the funny goings-on. The final straw for one worker was when he saw the letters EG appear in the dust at the side of him. Strangely enough, this is how Nell Gwynn, who is said to have spent time in the building, generally signed her name, although some claim that there are also associations to the girl Charles Dickens described as Little Nell, at what was then known as the Unicorn. People have even claimed that Charles Dickens and his mother, who spent time at nearby Tong where she worked, have been seen walking into the building.

Perhaps one of the most unusual occurrences to happen in this building is the following strange phenomenon. In 1997 I had just written a book about all the ghosts and phantoms of central England and was working and filming with

Naughty Nell's, Shifnal.

The author in the Great Chair, Naughty Nell's.

BBC Midlands *Today* at Naughty Nell's. The camera crew decided it would be a great visual presentation to burn one of my books on one of the hot plates of the cooker and film it in flames, and it did look quite brilliant on television that night.

After filming they made sure that nothing at all remained of the burning book, all electric appliances were switched off and absolutely nothing could have started a fire. However, exactly where the book had been burned, a fire started in the middle of the night that caused some damage to that part of the building, which was quite unexplainable. To this day, staff at the pub say that whenever Mr Rudge is angry, a smell of burning becomes present. This is a true story, and in my opinion, one of the scariest cases I have had to investigate.

The Poor Labourer, Snedshill

A very strange ghost story is told in the area of Snedshill of the vision of a man known by the name of 'the poor labourer', or sometimes 'the starving gentleman', dressed in ragged clothes. Legend has it that the ghost is of a man who visited the town looking for work but fell ill and could not maintain himself. He died in the Shifnal Workhouse shortly after arriving in the Snedshill area. Does his spirit still return searching for work or sustenance?

I think what is unusual about this particular ghost or spirit is that people see different visions. I think perhaps that there is more than one ghost that is witnessed. Carol Smith, a lady who is sensitive to such things, told me that on one occasion she tried to communicate with the man and that he actually thanked her for her advice. This would lead me to believe that it is a spirit energy rather than just a ghostly sighting.

The Wrekin

The old and ancient Wrekin Wakes was always held on the first Sunday in May and tended to be the highlight of the year for the local residents. One of the special events would see the farm labourers and the mining community involved in various games and activities for the right to claim the possession of 'the hill', and a tug-of-war, fist-fights between various champions from the agricultural and mining communities, and many other games would take place, alongside all the other traditional games and activities of the fair.

It is said that ancient rites once took place on the Wrekin and that one of the particular areas used was a bare rock at the very top or summit, in a hollow known as the Cuckoo's Cup or Raven's Bowl. This place is strangely always full of water, which ancient sages and wise men and women claimed came about from miraculous means and meant that all the creatures that lived there, particularly the birds and specifically the cuckoo, would always have water available.

It was also said that if you tasted the water it would be beneficial to your health. I do not recommend that you do this today, and if you do so, it is at your own risk. Legend also says that if a young girl touched the water then made her way down the steep hillside, and then went through a tight gap in the rock known as the Needle's Eye without looking back, then she may well, at the end of her journey, meet her true love. However, if she did look back then she would remain a maiden forever.

Other stories that are told about the Cuckoo's Cup, which are not so pleasant, say that if you are there at dusk you may well see the spirit of a large bird, or perhaps meet the large gentleman in the frock coat who will step forward and place a hand on your shoulder. Many other strange stories are told of the Wrekin, including the ghosts of black dogs, witches from yesteryear, and perhaps most strangely of all, an albino fox with red glowing eyes which screams at you before vanishing into thin air.

A group of teenagers had a frightening experience one evening while using a Ouija board. They claimed most strongly and collectively that when one of them asked the question when they would die, a figure whom they believed to be the Grim Reaper appeared before them. I don't believe the teenagers were lying but I do believe this was more likely from their own imagination.

Many professional mediums such as myself advise against the use of Ouija boards and one of the main reasons for this is that people tend to ask these sorts of questions but then experience a scary answer or vision such as this. I am sure it is from their unconscious mind or a sort of creation of a hypnotic experience. Having said that, the Wrekin can certainly be a most unusual and spooky area, especially outside of daylight hours!

Trench

Gareth told me of a very interesting experience he had while walking around the area as a young boy looking for rabbits on wasteland. In the company of his two dogs, the younger one looked up and started to bark. In the distance Gareth saw an old man in a long brown coat like the farmers used to wear. He had on a flat cap and looked relatively normal. Gareth said hello to the old man. The man turned and looked towards him but walked on with no

real acknowledgement. Walking on a little further, Gareth kept a lookout for him, but the man had completely disappeared. It seems that he must have been the ghost of one of the many farmers that operated in Telford, perhaps even being pre-Victorian and wearing the farmer's frock coat popular in this area in the old Salopian days. Then again, if the ghost looked Gareth's way, perhaps he was having a glimpse into the future. Anything is possible in my view.

Overley Hall, Wellington

The building at one time was a home and centre for the disabled. During this time, staff would often report seeing ghosts, including a tall gentleman in a cap, a little girl dressed either in white or green, and a figure of an older lady in a pantry hat who seemed to be dusting away, quite unaware of anyone being able to see her. Some people also tell the story of hearing little children who play in the tower at Overley Hall, laughter and squeals of delight that, although pleasant, could also be incredibly spooky if you had to go there on your own.

New Church Road, Wellington

Sarah emailed me about the house where she and her husband live in New Church Road in Wellington – a Victorian terrace which she believes was built around the 1880s. They are very happy there and don't feel at all uncomfortable by any of the presences they have experienced. There is also a church across the bottom of the gardens of the row of terraces, and many gravestones are propped up against the wall. These were moved when the graveyard was being cleared.

The Wrekin.

Ouija board.

During the last seven years they have had what Sarah describes as several 'visitors' that have been seen in the bedroom, dining room, hall and lounge, by herself, her husband and friends. Sarah says she often saw a little girl standing by the front door, but hasn't seen her for some time.

Her son, who was about five at the time, told her he could see a man on the path in front of the house, and on one occasion, as a friend who had visited opened the door to leave, she exclaimed, 'Oh my gosh, something has just run past me!' She told Sarah it was a feeling of something rushing past rather than actually seeing anything, but thought it seemed like a child.

Sarah says that on another occasion she woke in the night and saw a woman standing at the bottom of the bed dressed in what looked like clothes from the 1970s or '80s. She says, 'I saw her clearly, she was dressed in a puffy sleeved blouse and beige waistcoat and was wearing large-framed glasses. She seemed to be looking at me as though she wondered what I was doing there. But I didn't feel at all concerned and I went straight back to sleep.'

On another occasion, Sarah was in the attic when she happened to glance down through the hatch and saw a man dressed in a suit walk right through the loft ladder and disappear. One Christmas, when their nieces visited, one of the girls who was about eighteen at the time, commented to them, 'I couldn't live here, it's haunted!' A bit later they took some pictures of the family gathering and a huge orb was seen next to their niece who was sitting on the settee.

A friend of the family who comes to feed the cat when they are on holiday always comments on how spooky the house feels. The neighbours also claim to have seen or sensed things, and it would seem that the same woman who appeared to Sarah also visited the house three doors down about the same time, to the man who lived there, but he said she looked as though she was halfway through the floor.

The man who lives next door to Sarah told her that one night he saw a woman standing at the bottom of his stairs, looking up as though she was trying to work out how to get to the upstairs rooms. Another neighbour who lives a couple of doors away from her. claims that her furniture gets moved around on a fairly regular basis.

Another friend, Roxanne, who lives five doors up from her in the row, says a little girl haunts her house, and, although she has never seen the child, her sister has. Sarah wonders if it is the same child that used to visit her home.

Other neighbours, Jenny and Ray, who used to live in the end terrace but who now live opposite, say the cottages are very haunted. They remember when a ghostly woman dressed in clothes from the Victorian period used to visit them, who actually smiled and nodded at Ray on one occasion, before disappearing. They also had an incident where all the plates fell off the wall one after the other but they, like Sarah, never felt uncomfortable in their home.

Jenny and Sarah have a theory that all the hauntings that take place could be something to do with when the graveyard was cleared in the early 1970s. Sarah says that one evening her husband was returning home when he saw what looked like a monk who turned and started to run after him.

Another friend, whilst out riding on his bike, saw what he thought looked like a monk round the back of the shooting range at the Wrekin. He said that for some reason he got off his bike and started to run away. He can't explain why he did that, but he wouldn't go back for the bike and had to get his dad to collect it for him.

On another occasion, Sarah's mother told her she had been to a place called Eton Constantine, which is just round the corner from where they live, and saw a farmer leaning on a five-bar gate, who doffed his cap to her and smiled. She says she was just thinking how friendly the locals were when he dissolved in front of her eyes.

Sarah says that even though they have all these ghostly goings-on, she absolutely loves the feel of the place and wouldn't want to leave her home for anything.

The Buckatree Hotel, Wellington

The Buckatree Hall, now a hotel, was at one time used as a hunting lodge for Lord Forrester and has always had a history of strange goings-on. Perhaps the most unusual recurring haunting here happens if your car breaks down, where a mechanic seems to appear from nowhere in the car park or on the road approaching the hall and gets you on your way.

Another visitor to the hotel once claimed that a ghost, a beautiful lady in evening dress, had warned him not to drive his vehicle that evening and then vanished before his eyes. The storyteller says he presumes she must have been warning him that something bad would happen if he did, but he cannot say for sure if her prediction would have come true, for he decided to heed the warning and did not drive – so perhaps a bad accident was indeed averted.

Wellington

Mr Stirling wrote to me with his story, which is a very spooky one, I have to say. His experience occured in 1947 when, as a boy, he lived in a five-storey terraced house in High Street, Wellington which was owned by a family who lived across the road. His parents told him later that when they had gone to look at the property they had heard the story of a girl's head being found in the fire oven. This was an old-fashioned style cooking grate which had an oven either side of the fire and movable arms with hooks on for frying and boiling over the fire.

When they moved in, Mr Stirling shared a room with his brother on the third floor, but, in June of that year, he was moved into a room on the fifth floor which was situated near the front of the house. The windows were barred, so they could only be opened a little way to let in fresh air. The children always went to bed at 6.30 p.m. and their bedroom doors were locked at night.

Everything was fine until the end of September when Mr Stirling went to bed as normal and fell asleep. However, at about 11.30 p.m. that night he woke up very cold and was aware of the presence of someone or something in the room with him.

Suddenly, the door that was locked burst open as if someone was in a hurry or in a vile temper. There was a six-drawer chest that was full of clothes at the bottom of his bed and the drawers were inexplicably dragged open. The clothes started to fly all over the place as though someone was looking for something but could not find it. Then the same thing happened with the wardrobe.

Mr Stirling says that at the bottom of his bed he could then see a very dark figure wearing a black cloak and black pork pie hat with very piercing eyes; he was unshaven and had no teeth. The vision started to lift its arm and he could see he had something in his hand.

By this time, with the hair standing up on the back of his neck, Mr Stirling had summoned enough courage to leap out of his bed and run through the door, which

The author at the Buckatree Hall, Wellington.

Buckatree Hall.

was still open, and down to his parents' room which was on the first floor, shouting for help.

His father opened their bedroom door asking how he had got out of a locked room and what was wrong with him. He told him what he had seen and they went back up to his bedroom where the door was now shut and locked again. His father unlocked and opened the door and looked into the room; he saw all the clothes scattered everywhere. He commented that there was a funny smell in the room and Mr Stirling was moved back into the bedroom over the landing with his brother.

A week or so later they had a lodger who was given the room Mr Stirling had slept in on the fifth floor. As far as he knows, no one had told the lodger about what had happened, but, at the end of October, the same thing happened to him and, although he had been drunk, he told Mr Stirling's mother that someone had been in his room and the clothes out of the drawers had been thrown about everywhere.

At the end of November, the lodger was woken and the same thing happened to him again. This time, however, he was sober, and just after midnight he told them he was leaving straightaway. He was visibly shaking and was as white as a sheet.

Mr Stirling says that they lived in the house until 1950 and these disturbances only seemed to happen at the end of September, October and November – and then stopped until the same time the next year. His father told him he always put unwanted visitors in there from September onwards to get rid of them. Even their cat and dog used to be terrified and would bolt out of the room as fast as they could if they were put in there for any reason. After they moved out, the house was turned into a shop and used until the late 1960s when it was demolished to make way for new housing. But do these occurrences still take place in the area? It's an interesting thought, isn't it?

Trench Crossing, Wellington

Many years ago, an awful accident happened at the Trench Crossing when a poor man was beheaded on the railway line. Could this be the reason that for many years afterwards people reported seeing the various visions of a torso, legs, feet, and other body parts? People have even reported such events in the late evening to the authorities, yet, when investigations have taken place, nothing unusual has been found – certainly not body parts.

It may have nothing at all to do with the aforementioned accident but it is the sort of thing that could cause a replay in the ether of that terrible scene to those with the sensitivity or natural psychic ability to tune into the past. And this is where Barry told me of his experience of seeing a man in this area, describing him as being rather like the actor Humphrey Bogart, in long coat and hat, who appeared before him and then just as quickly dissolved into thin air.

The Cock Hotel, Wellington

The Cock Hotel in Holyhead Road is a most interesting building with an equally interesting history, for at one time it fulfilled the role that many old pubs originally provided in Shropshire – as a coaching inn. The hotel is also famed for its quality of drinks.

An unusual haunting has been reported on several occasions outside the Cock. Some people describe it as the vision of horses and carriage, which one might expect to see from shades of yesteryear, but, rather

Cock Hotel, Wellington.

Funeral cortege.

more unusually, they are the type of black horses and carriage that would have been used for funeral purposes in days of old.

The Swan Hotel, Wellington

The Swan Hotel in Watling Street has a very interesting story that was told to me by a man who stayed there at one time and had been to play golf on a nearby course, enjoying a good day's sport which had only been marred by losing a golf ball during a close game he had been playing with his friend. They searched everywhere but the ball was nowhere to be found.

Returning to his hotel room later that night, the man saw a golf ball lying on the floor. Adamant that his friend was playing a trick on him he laughed the experience off, but didn't find it funny the next day when a local told him that other people who had played on the golf course had had the same experience. For all that, he insisted the Swan was a great place and the spirits from behind the bar were most excellent!

Wellington Spiritualist Church.

Wellington Spiritualist Church

Jean told me one night that when she had attended Wellington Spiritualist Church, she had received a very interesting message from the medium visiting the church that evening. Apparently the medium had pointed to Jean and said, 'I want to come to you, my dear. Do you understand a man who owned a German Shepherd dog and smoked a pipe? He seems to be telling you to be a little careful about where you walk, and have you been having a problem with your legs at all?'

Jean replied, 'Well, as a young man my husband smoked a pipe but I don't ever remember him having a German Shepherd dog and I'm not really having a problem with my legs at all.'

'Well, said the medium, 'Just be mindful of the message I have given you and I'll leave it with you.'

Later that week, Jean decided to look through some old photographs and found an old faded picture of her late husband, Harry, during his war service overseas and there, indeed, was a picture of him smoking a pipe and with a German Shepherd dog at his side. Pleased by this, she thought she would take a few flowers to his grave that day. Approaching the entrance to the church, she noticed a lot of roadworks and various building tools, materials and equipment on the pavement which would have made it difficult for her to go into the churchyard. However, undaunted, she started to make her way round the obstacles to go in. Just as she did this she caught sight of a large dog from the corner of her eye that ran by, very much like a German shepherd. It caused her to pause for a moment and, right in front of her, was a hole that she could easily have put her foot into.

Did Jean receive a message from the other side that day in Wellington Spiritualist Church that saved her from injuries to her legs? And was it the spirit of her late husband's dog that had drawn close to save an accident?

Today, Jean feels quite sure her husband lives on the other side, believing it most likely that the dog is with him too. Not all ghost stories are scary; some tell of experiences that have saved people from injuries and misfortune, it seems.

Wenlock Priory

There is a very interesting ghostly vision seen here of a nun who walks in the vicinity of the priory, being followed by what appear to be two Viking warriors. Some report that this is all that is seen, although other sources say they have seen the development of this vision a little further and this poor lady of religious order is thrown to the ground and axed to death. If this happened at some time in history then it it is certainly the sort of situation

Wenlock Priory.

that would create a replay of her final awful moments in this world.

White Ladies Priory

Well-known Telford man, Bert Meek, told me of an unusual experience he had some years ago when riding past White Ladies Priory. Apparently, young people in those days, perhaps the 1940s or '50s, used to claim that if you laughed out loud in the centre of the ruins it would echo back to you.

Bert was on his own and decided he would try such an experiment, and laughed out loud, but, in his own words, left the area pedalling like mad and in a great hurry when the ghostly giggles of what sounded like several young girls echoed back at him!

Were they real girls playing a trick on him? Bert admits that this is a possibility, but then asks what happened to the echo of his laugh then, for that didn't sound at all that day.

Willey

The churchyard at Willey is haunted by Tom Moody, a horseman of great repute, who at one time worked for Lord Forrester of Willey Hall as the whipper-in (a whipper-in is someone who assists the huntsman during the hunt for foxes and other quarry). As head whipper-in, Tom would have also had a pack of hounds, a typical responsibility for those at Willey Hall in the eighteenth century. An expert horseman would be required to ride alongside the pack and in an around the course, ensuring no dogs strayed into private quarters. As whipper-in, this duty also fell on Tom Moody.

Nearing his death, Tom issued Lord Forrester with specific instructions as to where he should be buried, telling him: 'When I die, I wish to be buried at Barrow, under the yew tree, together with my whip, boots and spurs.' There were also other specific private instructions which Lord Forrester duly followed; two of his favourite hounds were to be brought to the grave to mourn his passing, and also three loud 'halloos' were to be shouted over his body to make absolutely certain that he was dead – Tom was terrified of the idea of being buried alive.

To this day, some say that in and around the country areas of Willey, Tom is still seen racing his horse across the open land and jumping hedges. But there is a link to Madeley too. Two men who had been out on the town for the evening, and had stayed behind at one of the pubs after hours, both claim to have seen the shades of Tom Moody and his horse ride through the town centre. Being Shropshire lads, they knew the story of Shropshire's whipper-in quite well and had seen pictures of the great horseman. It seems that he must have covered a much larger area of Shropshire than can be imagined and perhaps the two men saw a ghostly vision of Tom and his horse.

This was a story I always wondered about until a young lady told me the same story in 2009 of a similar horseman riding by; but was it Tom Moody? That is the ghostly question.

The Ghost Hunter's Toolkit

Something that you must have if you are to successfully investigate the paranormal, according to any parapsychologist or those interested in looking for ghosts professionally or with an amateur interest, is a completely open mind. This is of great importance and I can only say to you that whenever I have been involved in this kind of research accompanied by the type of individual or group who believe before they begin that they are not going to see, sense or find anything at all that could be considered paranormal, then they generally do not.

By the same principle, you should not undertake such investigations convinced that you will see something. This constitutes an open invitation to your mind and the unconscious levels to begin to play tricks on you, leading you to see and hear things that are not there. Also, be very careful not to insist that something is paranormal before all investigations have taken place to see if it is something that can otherwise be explained.

What I would suggest to the reader is this: if you are actually interested in finding out about ghosts in Telford, why not consider getting together a little ghost hunter's kit that would help greatly in finding out whether or not somewhere really is haunted. People may suggest you need things such as meters to measure electro-magnetic field changes, heat sensing cameras, special thermometers, and a whole plethora of fancy equipment that, in my experience as a ghost hunter, is really of very little use. The real necessities are simple, everyday items which you can gather generally from around your home or local hardware store.

One exception to the rule of equipment is you do need a good camera, and really this should be a 35mm camera which, if at all possible, has an infra-red lock on it. Photographs produced with digital cameras today can so very easily have pictures manipulated, that almost no self-respecting investigator of the paranormal has any interest in them. Also, just use a very simple camcorder but preferably one that can film in quite dim light. You don't need an expensive camcorder, and again I must inform you that most of the so-called orbs that are produced and presented as ghosts or other unusual phenomena, are actually no more than the usual dust particles in the air that are picked up by most camcorders when recording in the dark.

So, below is a very simple kit for you to get together, which I suggest would be more than acceptable to any ghost hunter in Telford, or anywhere else for that matter, together with a simple explanation of their uses and what you can do with them to check out ghosts and haunted buildings.

A Ghost Hunter's Toolkit

Notepad
Pen and Pencil
Retractable ruler
12in ruler
Watch – digital, with a nightlight
A good magnifying glass
Spool of black cotton
String
Tape-recorder
Contact adhesive – 1in tape
Powerful torch
A good thermometer
Packet of chalks
Talcum powder and 1in paintbrush
Pencil sharpener
Camera – built-in powerful flash
Video camera
Spare batteries for everything!

A notepad, and pens and pencils, are vital for making notes of anything that happens. Note exactly and absolutely factually any occurrences or sounds that are heard. Also note whether they were witnessed by someone else apart from you. Time and date them precisely.

You will find the magnifying glass that I have included in your kit of immeasurable use when looking at footprints and handprints. They may be invisible to the human eye but you will see them through your glass. It can also be used for examining traces of post-ghostly substances left behind.

The talcum powder and the paintbrush can also be very useful in conjunction with the magnifying glass. For example, if you shake the talc onto a cupboard, a chair, or perhaps a table or anything with a polished surface, then gently blow it away, it will leave impressions of prints, natural or supernatural, that are there. Now, should that print or prints not match any of those of the residents or visitors, you've got your first winner and you're learning the tricks of the trade of ghost hunting!

Now let's move to your chalks – you can use them to mark around movable objects, such as chairs or table legs, which have perhaps been reported to move around on their own. It may involve a long sitting on your part but if you have chalked it and it moves, you've got another winner haven't you?

The string, self-adhesive tape and cotton are for securing and sealing doors and windows. Far and away the best of the three, in my opinion, is the self-adhesive tape. For example, use about four or five pieces cut at about 3in and place them on the doors and frames which are reported as self-opening; set up your watch; the evidence of any breakage of the tape will be obvious.

A tape-recorder is also a most useful tool for anyone researching the existence of ghosts and should accompany you on every enquiry if at all possible. I would also suggest that you buy some extra batteries for it – the type that can be recharged time and time again. (Actually you should always carry a spare set of batteries for everything). They are an excellent investment and I do suggest that your tape-recorder should be on record at all times. However, be on your guard, for there is usually a natural explanation for most sounds.

Investing in a good camera is absolutely vital. I stress good rather than expensive and the fewer requirements for adjustments of controls, the better. It should incorporate an infra-red focus lock if at all possible, and, at the time of writing this article, the type of camera I have described can be purchased for less than £100. This is indeed the simple type of camera I use, and I find the infra-red lock and built-in flash invaluable at night.

A video camera is also an excellent piece of equipment to take on any investigation with you, but I do suggest that you explain to the supplier exactly what you want to use it for; some video cameras in my experience are much better than others for filming in the dark.

If you want more technical equipment, the following is a list of items that might prove useful to you above and beyond the simple kit I have suggested.

Electro-magnetic field detector (often referred to as EMF Meter) – is a piece of equipment that can detect the presence of electro-magnetic fields. There are many today who believe these fields can be caused by ghosts and can be picked up around haunted buildings, but do remember they also pick up measurements from televisions, electrical wiring, and other equipment, so keep this in mind if you use them. Also get one where the measurement is displayed for you, 2.5 to 2.10 milli-gauss or one that has a needle that gives a reading. You really want one that displays in the dark too. The very cheap ones that just beep or flash red or green when a ghost is allegedly present is not much use to you.

A 35mm camera – would really be the advised piece of equipment even over digital cameras. Anyone who examines your photographic evidence of ghosts will tend to be less prepared to accept it in digital format.

Use the very best film you can afford; my personal recommendation would be Kodak Gold 400 speed film, which gets the best all-round results in my view, although some favour 800 or 200 speed film. One problem you should be aware of is that pictures taken at night or in the dark with very fast speed can be quite grainy and unclear. You may wish to take advantage of using infra-red film but note that although it can be an excellent way to work at haunted sites, it can be quite expensive to purchase and these days very expensive to develop too.

A digital thermometer – will give you the capability of measuring such areas as cold spots. If you do get one, one that has a highest and lowest temperature memory and an alarm too would be the best to purchase. A better, but more expensive option, would be a thermal scanner which uses infra-red technology to immediately register temperature changes at a distance; not a cheap item, but a piece of equipment that can be extremely useful.

A night-vision camera – if you can afford one, this works in much the same way as equipping your ordinary video camera with a night-vision scope which will record light and the way it changes much more accurately, and even picks up light that you cannot see with your own eyes. Many parapsychologists today use night- vision scopes. They probably have their uses, perhaps in a dark churchyard or unlit lane, but they are pricey items that some people consider not really worth purchasing if you cannot afford the very best.

Thermal imaging scopes – can be used to measure temperature changes that happen in front of you and they will also let you have the ability to actually see what your thermal scanner sees, making use of infra-red technology. Not only will you be able to look on a cold spot, you would actually be able to see the form and shape it takes. Again, expensive equipment, but if you are serious about ghost hunting, this proves a very valuable item.

Digital tape-recorders – these have now become the must-have item for recording electronic voice phenomena and no one could really discount their value. Very large audio files can be stored on these little machines and the quality is brilliant, though personally I always like the old standard audio tape-recorder and separate microphone to be used as well, but then that is probably me being the traditionalist.

Motion detectors – can be a useful piece of equipment if used in the right hands and of good quality. They will certainly tell you if there has been movement somewhere where it should not have taken place. These sorts of things can be useful when set up across a room, corridor, or even stairs, and allow you to check out and monitor quite large spaces with just one simple-to-set-up device. They have certainly become a lot cheaper to buy now and can be a very useful ghost hunter's tool, especially for indoor work.

I advised you at the start of this chapter to get together a simple toolkit which I outlined. I still stand by this as the basic equipment that you will require in the early days of your interest in investigating the paranormal. As you get more serious about your work, perhaps you would like to add the other equipment and never-ending supply of things on offer to detect ghosts to your personal toolkit. Good luck to you, and I wish you happy ghost hunting!

Bibliography

BOOKS

Bradford, Anne & Roberts, Barrie, *Midland Ghosts & Hauntings* (Quercus, 1994)
Bradford, Anne, *The Haunted Midlands* (Brewin Books, 2006)
Burne, Charlotte S. and Georgina F. Jackson *Shropshire Folklore* (Privately published, London, 1891)
Frost, Allan, *Death and Disaster in Victorian Telford* (AJF Publications, 1995)
Scott-Davies, Allan, *Haunted Shropshire* (The History Press, 2009)

NEWSPAPERS

The Shropshire Star
The Wolverhampton Express & Star

OTHER

Wikipedia Encyclopedia

Other titles published by The History Press

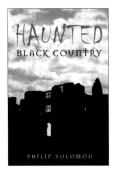

Haunted Black Country
PHILIP SOLOMON

This chilling collection of true-life tales covers the whole of the Black Country, reve
many accounts that have never before appeared in print. Compiled by the *Wolverham*
Express & Star's own psychic agony uncle, Philip Solomon, it contains a terrifying ra
of apparitions, from poltergeists and ghosts to ancient spirits, silent spectres, haunted
buildings and historical horrors. This comprehensive collection will delight anyone w
an interest in the darker side of the area's history.

978 0 7524 4882 4

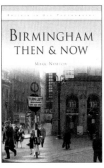

Birmingham Then & Now
MARK NORTON

Take a fascinating and nostalgic visual journey back to 1960s Birmingham to witness
much-loved Bull Ring, the grand city-centre buildings that were demolished to mak
way for the 'modern' city, and the streets and courts that were swept away during the
last fifty years of development. Mark Norton, author of *Birmingham Past & Present: In*
Father's Footsteps, presents many previously unpublished pictures, along with thoughtf
and detailed captions that provide a new insight into the ever-changing city.

978 0 7524 5722 2

Hanged at Birmingham
STEVE FIELDING

Until hanging was abolished in the 1960s, Birmingham's Winson Green Gaol was the
main centre of execution for convicted killers from all parts of the Midlands. Its histo
began in 1885 with the execution of Henry Kimberley, who had shot dead a woman
Birmingham pub. Over the next seventy-five years there were many more, including
poisoner 'nurse' Dorothea Waddingham and child-killer Horace Carter. Illustrated wi
over 50 pictures, this book tells of some of the country's most infamous criminals.

978 0 7524 5260 9

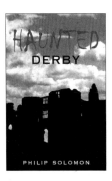

Haunted Derby
PHILIP SOLOMON

This creepy collection of true life tales takes the reader on a tour through the streets,
cemeteries, alehouses and attics of Derby city. Drawing on historical and contemporary
sources and containing many tales which have never before been published, it unearths
chilling range of supernatural phenomena from poltergeists to victorian spirits. This bo
will delight anyone with an interest in the supernatural history of the area.

978 0 7524 4484 0

Visit our website and discover thousands of other History Press books.

www.thehistorypress.co.uk